Kingdom Building in the Meantime

A Devotional for Holding on to God's Promises

Alicia J. Lewis

WESTBOW
PRESS®
A DIVISION OF THOMAS NELSON
& ZONDERVAN

Scripture taken from the Holy Bible, NEW INTERNATIONAL VERSION®. Copyright © 1973, 1978, 1984 by Biblica, Inc. All rights reserved worldwide. Used by permission. NEW INTERNATIONAL VERSION® and NIV® are registered trademarks of Biblica, Inc. Use of either trademark for the offering of goods or services requires the prior written consent of Biblica US, Inc.

Scripture taken from the King James Version of the Bible.

Scripture taken from the New King James Version. Copyright © 1979, 1980, 1982 by Thomas Nelson, Inc. Used by permission. All rights reserved.

Scripture taken from the Holy Bible: International Standard Version® Release 2.0. Copyright © 1996-2012 by the ISV Foundation. ALL RIGHTS RESERVED INTERNATIONALLY.

NET Bible® copyright ©1996-2006 by Biblical Studies Press, L.L.C. http://netbible.com All rights reserved.

Scripture quotations taken from the Holy Bible, New Living Translation, Copyright © 1996, 2004. Used by permission of Tyndale House Publishers, Inc., Wheaton, Illinois 60189. All rights reserved.

WestBow Press books may be ordered through booksellers or by contacting:

WestBow Press
A Division of Thomas Nelson & Zondervan
1663 Liberty Drive
Bloomington, IN 47403
www.westbowpress.com
1 (866) 928-1240

The book cover was designed by Elyria T. Clark of Etoshac Designs.

ISBN: 978-1-5127-1947-5 (sc)
ISBN: 978-1-5127-1948-2 (hc)
ISBN: 978-1-5127-1946-8 (e)

Library of Congress Control Number: 2015920871

Print information available on the last page.

WestBow Press rev. date: 1/4/2016

For You, Lord, as requested. May You be glorified in and through this work.

CONTENTS

INTRODUCTION

Waiting is an active stillness.

—Dr. Charles Stanley,
First Baptist Church, Atlanta

Have you ever had someone peer into your innermost being? Have you ever made eye contact with someone and realized that he or she really saw you? I recently had that experience. I greeted someone and could not help but notice how intently she stared at me. She smiled and held keen eye contact. When prompted, she said she could tell that I have been with God. When asked how that looks on someone (on me), she said that I had changed. She offered that I was more still and that it was a stillness that came from communing with and waiting on God. She indeed saw me.

I am in the meantime. The meantime is the time or season before the manifestation of God's promise. It is the period of time when we wait for His word to come to pass. I simply love how the word *promise* is defined. It is a declaration that one will do something specific. It is an indication of future success. God has given me His word that He will commit Himself to specifically bless me. How awesome is that? The Word gave me His word. And He has given it to you.

Unfortunately, many of us give up or, worse yet, fail to believe the promises God gives us. Similar to the parable in Matthew 13:3–8 about the good seed, our hearts are sometimes too rocky, shallow, or thorny to hold God's promises; therefore, we allow them to die. We allow spirits such as doubt, fear, insecurity, impatience, busyness, fatigue, and lack of faith to come and snatch God's word from our hearts. Has this ever happened to you? Have you ever given up on God by failure to keep before you His promises?

Promises are indications of future success. We must not forget this. If we are to live the lives God has promised us (Jeremiah 29:11), we must hold on to His word. This requires patient action. Kingdom building in the meantime is just that: it is a state of actively waiting for God's promise by putting our hands to the plow. It is faith in action as we wait for God's manifested promise. Seeds grow properly only when planted in good soil. Therefore, our hearts and subsequent actions must become pure and fertile in order to hold God's word.

My meantime season began over two years ago when God promised that I would marry. I believed Him. And I still believe Him and continue to hold Him at His word. This season has been difficult. In my waiting, however, I have held to His promise only through my growing relationship with Him and my resolve to build His kingdom as He instructs. God has given me specific instructions and opportunities in the meantime, just as I know He is giving you some. During this time, it is imperative that you attune your ears to His voice and heed His instructions. This devotional presents lessons I have learned and tools I have used during my meantime season to help you keep, protect, and grow seeds (God's promises) in your personal meantime.

The devotional may be read daily or weekly by chapter. Each chapter is named after a specific assignment God gave me to complete during this season. The chapters close with an offering to sit quietly before Him, while meditating on specific Scripture and probing questions. The purpose of the devotional's exercises is to help foster greater intimacy with God by allowing you to hear from Him and discover your meantime assignments. Therefore, you can read a chapter a day or a chapter a week, depending on how much you may need to reflect on and put into action things He places on your heart. Each devotion also provides an opportunity for you to share a promise you would like to make to God and prayers you may want to offer Him. If the space provided within each devotion is limited and you would like to also jot down promises He's making to you, use the Promise Pages in the appendix to capture this information. The appendix also provides a "Word to Stand On" section (foundational Scripture) for instances when doubt or other word snatchers come to attack your promise.

God may have promised you a job, promotion, child, business, healing, school opportunity, or deliverance from debt. It is my intention with this writing to encourage you to grow and sustain your faith in the meantime. Stand with me. Take a leap. Join me on this meantime journey from promise to manifestation.

CHAPTER 1

Lady in Waiting

And we know that all things work together for good
to them that love God, to them who are the called
according to his purpose.

—Romans 8:28 (KJV)

I did not grow up desiring to be married. I was not one of the many
girls I knew who had their weddings planned and children's names
chosen before they entered high school. I did not play with Barbie
and Ken dolls. But I must confess I absolutely loved my corn silk–
haired Cabbage Patch doll.

I can only assume I was indifferent in my attitude toward
marriage because I had not seen it modeled before me. Therefore,
I did not desire it. A single mom raised me; my parents divorced
when I was young. Other women in my family were also unmarried,
divorced, or separated from their husbands. The family member I
most wanted to be like was my widowed great-aunt, Ella, whose
husband died before I was born. I totally admired how she lived.
She traveled, earned a nice living, and wrote fat checks. I relished
receiving birthday and Christmas gifts from her; she gave me a couple

of hundred dollars on each occasion as a preteen. Undoubtedly, I wanted to be like Aunt Ella.

I did not have many boyfriends before or after college. I can name them on one hand. I "dated" a boy named Ollie a few days in elementary school; a guy named Brandon a couple of months in high school; a gentleman named Solomon a semester while in college; and a guy named Marvin a couple of years (on and off) during graduate school. That was it. I was always focused on my studies and activities. Dating was not a concern. Honestly, I did not see the point of dating if you were not going to eventually marry the person you dated.

I became interested in dating Marvin, however, after spending a lot of time with him. I was twenty-one years old and had known him since high school. I knew him pretty well. His best friend heavily pursued me while in high school, but I was not interested in him. I ran into Marvin—or, should I say, he saw me—one summer day while I was standing on a train platform after I had returned home upon graduating from college. He called out to me, and I was happy to see him. We started spending time together as friends. We ended up dating off and on during the two years I attended graduate school. I really liked Marvin and believe he also really liked me. He, however, was not interested in a commitment. I moved to Washington, DC, right after grad school for a summer internship. Shortly after I arrived, Marvin called and told me he wanted to be with his ex-girlfriend, whom he considered to be his soul mate. So that was it. Our relationship ended. I was single in a new city—the city I ultimately stayed in and still call home.

Marvin was the first and last guy I was serious about for a while. I was heartbroken. A while later, I met someone at a party held in a nightclub. He would be the best guy I had or have ever dated. OnYango rocked! He was secure within himself, patient, fun loving, courteous, giving, and such an overall gentleman. Before him, I had never met a guy who was okay with my celibacy; who would have my favorite music playing whenever I got into his car; who would refuse if I tried to pay for anything; and who I could call on to show up at the weirdest hour. But I was not ready for him.

After my experience with Marvin, I prayed and asked God to bring me a great guy. He did; OnYango was it. I really liked him, but I became anxious soon into our relationship. He got serious quickly. He invited me to Thanksgiving dinner with his family a few weeks after our first date—my heart raced. He was making plans for us months out in the future—my head spun. We would drive past homes, and he would ask my opinion of them. I tried acting nonchalantly in response. I knew how OnYango felt about me and that he would want to "put a ring on it." But I got nervous because this was entirely uncharted territory for me. What did that type of relationship look like? How was I to act and move into it? I did not have anyone to talk with about this who had been in a successful relationship. I was ill equipped and knew it. So I ended our relationship. He was devastated, and I missed him. He was my best friend. I just did not know how to handle a relationship that serious, especially not one going at an accelerated pace.

After my relationship with OnYango, I became the parent to a relative of mine (James is my uncle who I began raising when my grandfather was no longer able to raise him). I was twenty-seven years old and raising a male teenager whom I had relocated from my hometown to live with me. It was God's design and has proven to be an awesome experience—with a whole lot of awe, to say the least. So I did not date much in the eight years James was with me. (He's now away at college.) During that time, my life revolved around him, my faith and ministry, and my work. It was also during this time of ministry work that my heart opened and softened to the idea of being married.

God actually spoke to me about marriage six months or so before James went away to college. The "M" word was like an expletive in that it was coming at me from all directions. Everywhere I turned, someone (including a three-year-old) was talking to me about marriage. So I took heed when a friend randomly invited me to attend a multiday, Christian-based marriage workshop at her church. The Art of Marriage workshop, while open to singles, is primarily designed to help couples understand and work through God's design for marriage. Attendees watch a video series and break up into small groups to discuss different challenges and opportunities that marriage brings. The workshop also comes with a booklet for participants to read, which contains activities they can work on together. Following the three-day workshop, the church's relationship ministry launched a small group, which I attended, for participants to experience fellowship while discussing relationship concerns. I also read several Christian marriage-themed books over the next several months.

That season was beneficial. I digested a lot of useful information and reflected on what I had learned. The reflection time showed me how I'd erred in past situations, and it armed me with tips to improve my progress in future relationships. I incorporated some of the tools I learned into my everyday interactions with people, and I worked to resolve some past hang-ups with relatives. Simply put, I prayed a lot, forgave folks, and allowed God to work on me.

The next year, I attended my church's women's retreat. We invited a prophetess to join us as guest speaker. After picking her up from the airport, we sat down for lunch and she spoke to me about marriage. She said I would marry, described the man I would marry (both his physical and character traits), and urged me to purchase my wedding gown and pick out my colors and such because it would occur quickly and soon. When she finished speaking, I said okay and did not think much about it afterward. My spirit, however, began to nag at me sometime after the retreat. I needed to obey the prophetess's request. So over the course of a few months, I bought a couple of bridal magazines, thought through the type of wedding I desired, and bought a wedding gown. You read that correctly; I bought a wedding gown—husband unseen and nuptial date unknown. Talk about faith!

It has been almost a year since that retreat. It would be easy to doubt or get distracted as time moves on. God, however, continues to speak to me about marriage; He gives me random aromas. My pastor once likened the spiritual aroma we get from God to a physical aroma. In the natural realm, when we are hungry and a meal is being prepared, we smell the aroma and remain patient until the meal is ready. In my case, God's spiritual aroma is His way of reminding me about His promise. It keeps me faith-filled and strengthened until His promise is manifested. When my attention wanes or doubt tries to creep in, God sends a random yet timely word through someone to remind me of His promise. Therefore, when it comes to marriage, I am in the meantime.

Be Still, Be Open

Read Psalm 27:14, Psalm 31:24, Psalm 130:5, and Isaiah 40:31. Reflect on these Scriptures. Answer the questions and fulfill the requests provided below.

- What promise(s) are you waiting for God to fulfill? (If you have more than one promise, seek God in prayer for the order and His priority.)

- What is your attitude toward waiting?

- How are you waiting? What are you doing during the wait?

- What can you do to improve your waiting posture and attitude?

- Are you preparing yourself for His promise(s)? How?

- If not, how should you be preparing? What are some things you could be doing?

- Who and what are some resources you can tap into this week to help prepare you?

- Has God sent you some aroma? If so, describe it. How often does it come?

- If God has not sent you signs of His pending promise, seek Him in prayer about it.

- Journal your experiences this week.

Lord, I promise _____

_____

_____

Dear God, I thank You for Your awesome timing and for leading me to this resource. I pray that You will ready my heart for all that You will share with me during this season. Help me to become more patient with others and trusting of You. Strengthen my faith. Endear me to You and Your Word. Increase and improve our time of fellowship. Speak to me like never before. Allow me to experience You in a new way. Grant me clear instructions, and place before me the resources necessary to complete them. Groom me so that I might properly care for the release You are about to bestow upon me. It is in Jesus's matchless name that I pray. Amen.

CHAPTER 2

Don't Jump Just Yet

Do not be anxious about anything, but in everything
by prayer and supplication with thanksgiving let
your requests be made known to God.

—Philippians 4:6 NKJV

Have you ever wanted something to either end or move forward
so badly that you just could not help wanting to make it happen
yourself? Was there a car you wanted to purchase before you actually
had the funds to pay for it outright? Are you beyond ready to leave
your current job, and any other job just might do? Do you think you
have found your lifelong mate, although secretly you are not sure?
Are you considering ending a serious relationship without true cause?
Do not jump just yet.

I admit to having sincerely struggled with patience. Anyone who
has known me a good while knows this to be true. I cannot attribute
it to anything specific, but I can recall my earliest memory of being
nicely called impatient. My great uncle used to call me "Come
On." Apparently, that was the phrase I used at eight or so years of
age when spending time with him. Every summer, my grandfather,
Gran, and I would visit family in Kentucky. It was a treat. I would

stay with my great-grandmother Rose. Uncle George lived with her for a time before he died. He was blind, but that did not stop him (or me) from getting out. I guess I would always say "come on" to him because that is what he always called me. I would travel five hours with my grandfather to Kentucky and upon arriving, walk into my great-grandmother's house and Uncle George would say, "Uh oh, Come On is here." I loved Uncle George. He was my friend and walking buddy. We would walk around my great-grandmother's neighborhood and along Main Street to see the shops. I suppose I would urge him on when I was ready to go outside by using my favorite phrase, "come on." And as I said, it stuck.

I did not begin forming a personal relationship with God until I was in my twenties. It was not for lack of interest, but rather for lack of knowledge. I had not learned about (or even heard the term) having a "personal relationship" with God until then. Prior to joining my present church, my relationship with God consisted of going to church, serving in ministry, and praying when I needed Him to move on some issue in my life. I suppose my prayers to God were comparable to my requests to Uncle George, "Come on." Does this sound familiar?

Several years ago, the Lord transitioned me from one employer to another. The job change was all Him. If it had been up to me, I would have remained with my previous employer. But He had other plans. The culture of the new place was entirely different and took some time getting used to. I no longer worked fast-paced days in a highly politicized environment where tasks needed to be done yesterday. I stepped into Pleasantville. Have you seen the film by that title? I went from living in color to living in black and white. Do not get me wrong. The people at my new job were extremely nice, and the work was not difficult. That is why the place reminded me so much of the film. It was as if I had stepped back in time. Sadly, I knew within six months that I no longer wanted to work there. In fact, I hadn't wanted to interview for the job. I must have applied for it, but I really do not remember doing so. The first interview had gone well, but I hoped they would not call me back. Ha—no such luck! God woke me up that night and told me to write a thank you letter. "Really?" I asked Him. He said yes, and I wrote the letter. Not long afterward, I was asked to return for a second interview. I remember the conversation I had with God while getting dressed. I was whining to Him, "Do I really have to go?" He said yes, and I grudgingly went, landed the job, and remained there for four and a half years.

Do you hear from God? Or do you simply lodge complaints at His feet? Is your conversation with Him a combination of both? God was slowing me down and positioning me to spend time with Him. Over time, I prayed a lot more, read and studied His Word more, and sat still and listened for Him to speak. These activities were in addition to my routine church and Bible study attendance and my work in ministry. My relationship with Him grew more personal. It was not about "the work" and being of service, but about sincerely communing with Him. God was courting me. We did not just have dates, but we talked and listened to one another. I poured out my heart to Him, and He in turn poured His heart into me. I began to care about hurting His feelings and disappointing Him if I erred. I valued our relationship and placed it ahead of others, no matter the cost. And that is where things got interesting.

The Word of God is accurate when it says we war with our own selves (Romans 7:14–25). The spirit man (or conscience) wants to do what is right, but at times we are overtaken by and succumb to our flesh and earthly desires. We allow poor motives or our own selfish desires to lead us in ways that are contrary to God's Word, the Holy Spirit within us, or our basic good sense. While I knew God placed me in that job, I was beyond ready to leave. Sure, I was in prayer the full four and a half years, petitioning God to move ("come on"), listening to Him say no, and intermittently applying for jobs anyway. I wanted this season to end and a better one of my liking to start. It could not come fast enough!

Are you sometimes so stubborn, obstinate, or pig-headed that God has to close doors or seal others shut in order for you to get the message? I was. I have been there, done that, and have the T-shirt. I literally packed up my office in anticipation of getting a new job. I cannot say how many applications I sent out for other jobs, but no matter the number, God was in control and would not open those doors. I was teasing myself by dreaming up fantasies of how a particular new job would be.

> Casting down imaginations, and every high thing that exalteth itself against the knowledge of God, and bringing into captivity every thought to the obedience of Christ. (2 Corinthians 10:5 KJV)

I was causing myself to suffer by allowing my imagination to run wild envisioning my pretend newfound life. God had been telling me to sit down. I finally did. I surrendered and stopped fighting God and instead improved our relationship. I talked and challenged Him less and began listening and reflecting on His Word more. My vocabulary and demeanor changed. I no longer pleaded with God to "come on," but rather asked that His will be done.

Later on, I was led to take home those packed boxes in my office. I had a knowing within my spirit. I knew my time was coming to a close at that job. I had not been looking for work. I just somehow knew to take those boxes home, and I patiently waited on God for what would come. One day, in the midst of planning a work-related event, I emailed a colleague to inquire if she would recommend someone to speak at the event. She did not respond with someone's name. She did not answer the question at all. Instead, she alerted me to an open position on her team and asked that I call her to discuss it. I had received an unsolicited job offer. Talk about something falling into your lap! When an opportunity is yours (from God), it is yours. When God moves, He moves quickly. Within a week or so of speaking with my colleague, I interviewed with at least four people and received a formal job offer. One day I was patiently waiting on God to move, and the next day I was submitting my letter of resignation.

My word of counsel is this: don't jump into something major that you neither petitioned God for nor received His blessing on. Wait on Him (Psalm 27:14). Moving ahead in your own pig-headed strength will lead to negative consequences.

Be Still, Be Open

Read and reflect on the Scriptures given or referenced in the text above. Answer the questions and complete the requests made below.

- What have you been anxious about in the past?

- If you moved forward in error, what happened and what did you learn?

- Are you presently anxious about anything? How will you proceed this time around?

- How do you define surrender? How does your definition vary from God's definition?

Exercise: What do you desire from God? In my example, it was a new job. Seek God in prayer for what you should specifically request and/or look for in that particular area. For example, I had a vision for my next job, and I developed a short list of criteria. The criteria outlined my minimum requirements for any position I would come across. This list helped me narrow down options, and truth be told, the job God blessed me with met each of the criteria. That is how I knew to accept the job offer. Make sure your criteria are just as specific (Habakkuk 2:2). Place your list in a journal, in your Bible, on your home mirror, or somewhere that you can easily refer to it. Keep the list before you and use it, along with prayer, to identify God's choice. Be sure to surrender during the wait. Do not jump just yet.

- Journal your experiences this week.

Lord, I promise _____
_____
_____

Dear God, show me Your will and help me to yield to it. Remind me, Father, that surrendering is an active state of waiting on Your guidance and timing. Lord, during this time strengthen our relationship. Help me to continually cast down my own imaginations. Reveal Your thoughts to me and make them my thoughts. Show me Your ways and make them my ways. Father, give me specific instructions and the confidence to obey them. Move my heart to no longer *date* You, but rather to fully commit to You and Your word. Grace me with Your patience as You guide me into Your best. This is Your promise and I believe You will keep it. In Jesus's name I pray. Amen.

CHAPTER 3

Live In Purpose

The Lord Almighty has sworn, "Surely, as I have
planned, so it will be, and as I have purposed, so it
will happen."

—Isaiah 14:24 NIV

As mentioned earlier, I moved to Washington, DC as a single,
twenty-three-year-old woman. I was footloose and fancy-free. The
only commitment I had—outside of my relationship with God—
was to my employer. On top of that, I am an only child, which
meant I just had to occasionally check in with my mother back home
in Chicago. Life was good and fun. I enjoyed discovering a new city
and making new friends.

Two years after moving to Washington, DC, I purchased a
condo and was led to invite my ten-year-old uncle to stay with me
during a summer. James was sheltered, coddled, and had never
experienced city life and its myriad activities. I was a good niece. I
enrolled James into some neat camps, and he participated in many
first-time activities. Prior to his spending time with me, he had never
attended a baseball game or a theatrical play or visited an amusement
park. I sent for him the next summer, and we again explored the

city together. After that trip, James decided he wanted to move to Washington, DC and live with me. I was unaware that God had come to the same conclusion. They were in cahoots.

We understand that God has placed many gifts within us for His use (Romans 12:4–8). What we do not instantly know, however, is what gifts we are carrying and when they will be birthed. Rest assured, He will call us in His awesome timing, and all will be revealed when we avail ourselves to Him (1 Samuel 3:8–10). As for me, I was lying in bed some time later and suddenly *knew* that I was to permanently send for James. I had to prepare and so should you.

I immediately considered my environment. Was it conducive to raising a child? Is your environment favorable for God's promise and gift? I lived in a condo, and while it worked fabulously for me I would need space for a growing boy. I had to make room for my gift, and sure enough, God provided. I was in my car, returning home from a work meeting one day, when I passed a house with a for sale sign in the front yard. I do not know how or why, but the house caught my attention. I liked its location, and the neighborhood was quiet. I researched the house online and visited it a few times at night and during the day. I really stalked that house! One night, I drove through an alley that led to the home, parked, opened the home's gate, and walked onto the property. I peeked into a few windows to check the place out. I walked the property, claiming it aloud in Jesus's name. I took a friend who happened to be in town to see *my* house. After all of that, I finally contacted my real estate agent and bought and moved into the house. It was my house! Take heed. Prepare and/or change your surroundings for God's promise.

As a single woman, I also realized that there would be times I would not be able to relate to James. I needed to find a godly male mentor who could step in when necessary. I contacted one of the elders of my church who was acquainted with James and asked if he would serve as James's mentor. He agreed. Do you know someone who is mature and can help you care for your promise from God? Jesus instructed and poured Himself into the disciples for three years before returning to His father. We all need spiritual midwives and confidantes. Ask God to direct you to those from whom you might need assistance and make it happen.

When God places a seed in you, He will give you instructions on how to care for it (Judges 13:3–5). A few days before James came to live with me, I was given a list of items to discuss with him. The Lord wanted me to clearly understand and explain the purpose of James living with me. He also wanted me to outline God's (and my) expectations for him and the house rules, which I did. Be still; allow God to share your gift's purpose with you. He will share how it must be cared for and how He wants it to be used. His promise unto you is life, and it comes with great responsibility.

Most of the time, we think we understand what we are getting ourselves into when pushed into a new life experience. But honestly, there is always more than meets the eye, and it is often revealed after we jump in (Esther 2:12–14). God wanted and needed my lifestyle to change. Are there things about your lifestyle that need to change? I was used to working feverishly for the mayor of the District of Columbia, joining friends for dinner after work, and attending church on Sundays. Those times were over. Christians refer to time as either BC (before Christ) or AD (after Christ's death). Well, in my life it was either BJ (before James) or AJ (after James).

After James, my job, personal time, and worship habits changed. Everything had to change in order to appropriately care for God's gift. I was no longer able to work nonstop days and evenings; God moved me out of my District of Columbia government job and into a mommy job at a slower-paced company. I was no longer able to hang out with friends and coworkers for dinner in the evenings, because James needed me at home to assist him with homework and make him dinner. Prayer and intimate worship were no longer relegated to Sundays; my gift had me on my face nightly. It was hard. My life changed almost overnight as a result of this gift. There was no more *me;* it truly was all about my assignment (Ephesians 4:22–24). And it was costing me. But my newfound worship and His faithfulness carried me along. Be prepared for God to shift some things in your life. It will not always feel good, but it will develop necessary godly traits and habits in you and let loose the gift He has entrusted you with.

Be Still, Be Open

Read and reflect on each Scripture mentioned or those referenced in the text above. Answer the questions and complete the requests made below.

- Has God revealed to you His current purpose for your life?

- Are you living in His purpose? If not, why aren't you?

- Has He given you instructions on how to prepare for this purpose?

- What gifts or changes to your lifestyle are required to receive and care for His purpose?

- How far along are you in tapping into and developing these gifts?

- What lifestyle changes do you still need to make?

- This week, contact whomever God places on your heart to serve as a midwife to help you birth and prepare for His gift.

- Read Jeremiah 29:11, and afterward praise God for what He is doing in your life!

- Journal your experiences this week.

Lord, I promise _____
_____
_____

Dear God, thank You for loving and trusting me enough to design specific plans and purposes for my life. Father, show me and keep before me my current purpose in You. Soften my heart, Lord. Help me to obey. Reveal and continually remind me of the instructions You have for me during this time. Give me joy and patience as I execute each task before me. Keep my thoughts pure and my speech kind. Help me to speak positively to every situation I come across and act lovingly toward the mentor You give me. I thank You in advance for this time of preparation and for molding me into the fearless and wonderful creation You envision. In Jesus's name I pray. Amen.

CHAPTER 4

Discover What You Have and Teach Others

But we have this treasure in earthen vessels, so that the surpassing greatness of the power will be of God and not from ourselves.

—2 Corinthians 4:7 KJV

It was he who gave some as apostles, some as prophets, some as evangelists, and some as pastors and teachers, to equip the saints for the work of the ministry, that is, to build up the body of Christ ...

—Ephesians 4:11–12 NET

What are you working with? What do you have to give to others? If Jesus approached you for fruit, what would you have to offer? We may not often ponder our gifts and contributions to others, but we ought to in order to be purposeful and effective.

Sometimes, our talents find us; other times, people discover them or pull them out of us. Either way, it is important that we discover them and share them with others. Aren't you glad your hairstylist, nail technician, or dry cleaner found hers? Where would we be on days of special occasions without them? Who might you leave in a lurch until you discover and step into your gifts?

Teaching is the act of helping someone by imparting a gift or knowledge of a particular subject to him or her. Teachers are important because they help prepare people for their ultimate purposes. If we did not have teachers (well, good ones), our society and the body of Christ would be ill-equipped for the task before it. We would essentially be dead people walking and prey ripe for the kill.

I never thought of myself as being a teacher. I honestly did not give much thought at all to identifying or knowing my talents and gifts. I was just being. For example, I like music, so as a child I sang in the choir and played the hand bells in church. Singing in the choir stayed with me through college and adulthood. To this day, I still sing in church, but this time as a member of the praise and worship team. Again, I never saw singing as a gift I had. I was merely being me. That is one way gifts are manifested and seen.

I cannot fully recall how the gift of teaching was seen in me, but it was. My son, James, and I were in our dining room one day when he declared that I should teach. Maybe it was during homework time. I remember brushing him off because I was not interested in becoming a teacher. Some years later, he suggested it again, but this time, he thought I should teach within the church. Again, I brushed him off. But lo and behold, God must have been in agreement because I do serve now as a teacher in my church.

I began teaching youth Sunday school classes. Sunday school led to vacation Bible school (VBS). VBS led to occasional Bible studies. I liked it. I was gung ho at the outset about teaching. In fact, I created a syllabus my first time out because of all the ideas I had. Who knew? Apparently God did. After some time, my excitement began to wane because I no longer wanted to solely teach the youth. I wanted to teach the adults. I shared my interest with the head of my church's education ministry, but I was outnumbered by the other leaders who taught adult classes. I never mentioned this to anyone within the ministry, but I grew discouraged and bored. I began to see myself as the *junior* minister. I wanted to graduate to the big kids' table and teach the adults—and not just during an occasional Bible study.

Last summer, the education department was gearing up for vacation Bible school. I had already determined that I was not interested in teaching. I love the youth, but I no longer wanted to teach the youth VBS class. I arrived at church early one evening for prayer when volunteers for VBS were also meeting to divvy up classes by age group and receive their respective lessons. I sat near their meeting while waiting for prayer to begin. The volunteers received the age group they requested. The team, however, was one teacher short. They needed someone to teach the adult class. God is hilarious. There had never been a time when the adult class slot was not filled. Sure enough, I was asked to teach it and grudgingly accepted.

I came home and admittedly complained a bit because I did not want to teach vacation Bible school. I wanted to sit the season out and learn from others. I shared my frustration with James. He was confused. He quickly reminded me of how I had wanted to teach the adults for years and had now been given the chance. I could not see the forest for the trees. I was wrapped up in my feelings about not wanting to teach at all. I even expressed that my desire to teach the adults was in years past—not the present. It was then that James pointed out that God evidently wanted me to teach the adults now and not then.

God's timing surely is not ours. That is for sure. Needless to say, God was with me. I taught the adult VBS class, and it went well. Shortly afterward, my church's associate pastor asked me to teach a new class beginning in the fall called *How to Study the Bible*. It would be an adult class of my own! God is something.

Be open to opportunities that come your way to share your gifts. You will undoubtedly grow and have fun in the process of teaching, equipping, and encouraging others. Teaching is a joy fest all the way around. It is a gift that keeps on giving. So give!

Be Still, Be Open

Reflect on the following questions; answer them and complete the requests made below.

- Are you unsure of your gifts?

- Are there certain activities you gravitate to and do well in?

- Do you have skills you sometimes take for granted?

- Do others ask you to do, lead, or participate in certain tasks?

- Make a list of the gifts you are reminded of and discover while answering these questions.

Exercise: Take an online spiritual gifts test. There are several to choose from. Or, refer to the Resources section near the end of the book for a list of recommended spiritual gifts tests. If you are aware of your gift, contact an organization or person the Lord lays on your heart this week and teach and/or share what you know.

- Journal your experiences this week.

Lord, I promise ____
____
____

Dear God, thank You for equipping me to become a blessing to someone else. Remove all doubt, fear, and insecurities I may have about my abilities and gifts. Reveal new, undiscovered gifts that presently lay dormant within me, and put me in a position to display them for Your glory. Sharpen each of my gifts, and remove all hindrances to keeping them active or perfecting them. Thank You, Lord, for the hearts touched, souls saved, and lives changed, including my own. In Jesus's name I pray. Amen.

CHAPTER 5

Go to School

Shortly before dawn Jesus went out to them, walking
on the lake. When the disciples saw Him walking
on the lake, they were terrified. "It's a ghost," they
said, and cried out in fear. But Jesus immediately
said to them: "Take courage. It is I. Don't be afraid."
—Matthew 14:25–27 NIV

I have attended and completed both college and graduate school.
However, I want to attend law school. I cannot quite place the
moment when the desire came. It could have been while working
for the mayor of Washington, DC and realizing that I could totally
do what the attorneys around me did. Shucks, to be honest, I really
was doing it. Or, the desire could have come earlier.

It, however, was not until ten years later that the desire
resurfaced, and it was intense. I was actually going to step out and
do it. I spoke with colleagues who have their law degrees about their
experiences. I questioned them about the law school admission test
(LSAT) and if obtaining a law degree was worth it. I wanted to know
if they regretted the decision or if they would be where they are
today without the degree and law school experience. Based on their

favorable feedback and the hunger within me, I began researching law school programs. I contacted colleagues to write my letters of recommendation. I found LSAT prep classes and was about to enroll in one I preferred most.

While on a walk with my son, I mentioned my desire, the steps I had taken, and my intention to enroll soon in a class. I was extremely enthused (practically gushing), but he did not meet my level of excitement. In fact, he seemed lukewarm about the idea. I then shared my interest with my pastor who, to my surprise, also did not share my level of excitement. Admittedly, I allowed doubt to set in. Maybe I was trying to make something happen, and it was not what God intended for me. I shared my interest with two men whose spiritual insight and overall blessings I respect, and they were equivocally supportive. So, I did not register for the LSAT; neither did I enroll in the LSAT prep courses.

Not long after the lukewarm reception of my news, I began interviewing for a job at a university with a stellar law school program. *This is it,* I thought. I would land the gig and have them pay for law school. Perfect. One interview led to the next one. I felt confident, and the interviewer showed great interest. He gave me a tour around the office and mentioned that I would hear back from him in a couple of weeks. After not receiving word, I contacted the interviewer to inquire about the delay. He was upbeat as he apologized for the delay and assured me that I would receive word shortly.

"Shortly" turned into a few months. I figured I did not get the job. These days, potential employers are a bit rude. They do not routinely notify you if another candidate was selected in your stead for a position. But I did not want to give the employer the satisfaction of dodging the bullet by not telling me directly. I sent him an email asking that he confirm whether or not another candidate was hired. He responded that someone else indeed had been hired and was working in the role. It had been at least five months since I'd become gung ho about applying to law school. After not obtaining the university position, I no longer thought about law school.

Several weeks later, I was at church. The ministerial staff always prays together in the pastor's office before each service. I was in the sanctuary greeting and speaking with members of the church while the ministerial staff gathered to pray. Realizing I was delayed, I made my way to the pastor's office. As I approached the door, I heard him ask my whereabouts. His office door opened, and I said, "Here I am." I stepped in and proceeded to grab the hand of the person next to me to pray. Then the pastor said, "Alicia, you need to get your attorney's degree." I'm serious! Just like that. I told him that his response was weird, considering his lukewarm reaction when I shared my interest with him months earlier. He said a little something, we ministers prayed, and the service began.

After church service, I went to the store to buy an iron. A male cashier called me forward. He was annoyingly chatty. While trying to render payment, he was a bit nosy and asked about the type of work I did, the schools I had attended, and began talking to me about law school. He mentioned the same law school I wanted to attend and shared that he was presently taking an LSAT prep class. He suggested I join him. I paid for the iron and was about to walk away when he said, "I'll see you there," referring to law school. I just said, "Okay" and left.

Admittedly, I went home and reviewed LSAT prep classes online but did not register. Without recognizing the voice of God, I got super holy and felt I needed to pray first. Was this just two random people with the same thought, or was this God speaking through them? I needed to be sure. Six days later, a friend whom I had not spoken with in a while called me. During our chat, she mentioned that I put self-imposed limits on myself and that I am in a season of waiting, which lends itself to opportunities. Mind you, she led the conversation and said all of this without me telling her about my season or anything else. That is all I needed to hear. I went home and registered for the June LSAT exam and a three-month LSAT prep course that begins in a week and a half.

What am I saying? Apply to school if it has been on your heart and if God is in your corner. He will certainly be a lamp unto your feet and a light unto your path. He will make a way. I am expecting my ram in the bush because I do not intend to pay for law school. I am going to rock out on that LSAT. Believe it! I do.

Be Still, Be Open

Just as I believe God will make provision for me for law school, I believe He will make provision for your program of study. If He has placed this desire in your heart, He is simply waiting on you to push and birth it.

Read and reflect on Matthew 14:22–29. Answer the questions and complete the requests made below.

- Is there an academic or certification program God is encouraging you to pursue?

- Leap! Walk on water. Research program offerings in your area this week.

- Pray on the information and opportunity you come across. If God bids you to act, enroll this week!

- Journal your experiences this week.

Lord, I promise _____
_____
_____

Dear God, shroud me with Your boldness. Fill me with Your confidence. Speak so that I may know it is You. I lay my desire to continue my education before You. Lord, lead me to know Your will and move in it. I pray You will provide all the resources and open every door necessary to bring this opportunity to pass. Prepare my heart and mind and grace me with unmerited favor. Adorn me with wisdom and lead me with Your truth. I thank You for Your peace that surpasses all understanding as I patiently wait for the unfolding of Your plan. In Jesus's name I pray. Amen.

CHAPTER 6

Dance

Behold, I will do a new thing; now it shall spring
forth; shall ye not know it? I will even make a way
in the wilderness, and rivers in the desert.
—Isaiah 43:19 KJV

I am expressive. I talk with my hands. I find myself making random
voices while in the bathroom. When reading aloud, I am animated.
It is just who I am. When music comes on, I sway, rock, or sing
along. I think it comes from my grandmother. She is quite the same
way. She sings and is a hummer. I picked up these traits from her.

I remember being in my dining room one day a few years ago.
My son was with me. He is a member of our church's dance ministry
and suggested I join the team. I immediately shut down the idea by
saying something like, "I'm not doing that."

Sometime later, the dance ministry leader approached me about
joining the team. I must have considered it and agreed because I
danced with the team for a while. And I occasionally render my
services when asked or when God impresses upon me the need or
desire to dance. For instance, I woke up a few days ago to a spiritual
attack that upset me because it sought to tempt me and cause me to

sin. God gave me a song, and I am preparing to dance out a release as my affirmation to not go back and as my declaration that Jesus is my champion. Dance is ministry, not just for others, but for the vessel also. This is demonstrated in Jeremiah 31. In this text, God is coming to deliver and reclaim Israel. Upon hearing the news, the clans of Israel rejoice and praise the Lord.

> The young women will dance and be glad, young men and old as well. I will turn their mourning into gladness. I will give them comfort and joy instead of sorrow. (Jeremiah 31:13 NIV)

Dancing provides a spiritual release. But we must be careful about the spirit in which we dance and what we are releasing. Admittedly, I loved dancing in the world. Shucks, when my friends and I went out, I was the first person on the dance floor. Some people drank, others smoked, but I danced. On the dance floor is where you would find me and still will at an occasional birthday party or other festive gathering. Praise dance, however, came easily and felt natural, especially since I had an in-home choreographer. In hindsight, dancing was a great way for me to bond with James and to spend time with each other. It was also a means for us to share what God was saying to us with the body of Christ. We heard God and were in sync with our ideas and ministry. James would usually suggest a song, I would receive the vision for how it ought to be expressed, and we would work together on choreography. It was a great feeling of closeness—not only with James, but also with God. I greatly enjoyed ministering with my son in dance. And the Holy Spirit totally used us.

Prior to the dance ministry, I had never been fully overtaken or unaware of my surroundings as a result of the movement of the Holy Spirit. Immediately before ministering in dance, I am a wreck. When I know God is really going to show up and show out, I shake uncontrollably. This is how I know it is not about me and that I am merely a vessel for His use. I get so anxious and am in prayer for God to have His way. I pray that His will be done and received through the dance. I pray for a receptive audience. When I dance, I go someplace else. I do not see the congregation. I do not know exactly what I am doing, if the moves are accurate, or how I look. It is just the music, God, and me. And He definitely receives all the glory.

Be Still, Be Open

Reflect on Isaiah 43:19. Answer the questions and fulfill the requests made below.

- Are you willing to allow God to take you to another place in Him?

- Do you have the desire to dance for the Lord?

- Is He calling you to this or another ministry?

- Do it this week. Express your interest and join!

- Journal your experiences this week.

Lord, I promise _____

_____

_____

Dear God, thank You for being in total control and for having my best interests at heart. Thank You for Your supernatural covering. I love the love You show forth unto me. Give me Your joy and allow others I encounter to feel it. Renew my mind and help me to cast down all doubt and fear. Continue to allow me to abide in Your presence. Allow me to experience more of You. Thank You for drawing me closer to You. I give You all of me just, as You have given me all of You. For this I am eternally grateful. In Jesus's name I pray. Amen.

CHAPTER 7

Become a Mentor

No one lights a lamp and puts it in a place where
it will be hidden, or under a bowl. Instead he puts
it on its stand, so that those who come in may see
the light.

—Luke 11:33 NIV

It is true. Your gifts will certainly make room for you. We really
are living epistles before men and women. People do watch and pay
attention to how you and I live. They are sizing us up, inspecting us,
discovering our gifts, and making note of our attitudes in different
settings and situations. These observations happen in all settings. It
is as simple as being watched by a coworker and/or classmate, fellow
gym members and sports teammates, your kids' friends and their
parents, relatives, folks in ministry, or people you sit next to on your
routine commute. And trust me that when a need arises, they will
or will not approach you—based on their assessment of you. How
are you faring?

I attend a small church by today's standards. There may be
sixty people in attendance on any given Sunday. I liken church to
school. It gets smaller and easier to manage if you are involved. If

you participate in sports teams, dance troupes, and academic clubs, a large school becomes smaller because of your relationships. It is the same with church. You are better acquainted with others in ministry if you are active, rather than only attending Sunday service. Serving as church administrator, praise and worship team member, dance member, Sunday school teacher, minister, and occasional Bible study teacher helped me forge relationships with other church members. They size me up and tap me on the shoulder when a need arises. The need varies from a prayer, a ride to church, or an opportunity to chat over a meal to intercession, opening up my home, serving as an ad hoc seamstress, helping others manage their finances, and lending an ear and shoulder to cry on.

A family at church once went through a hard time. One of the parents suffered a health challenge, and the child needed someone. I am glad to have been the *someone* the child could turn to for assistance. Over a period of time, she called me very early in the morning or very late at night. I made myself available. We talked and prayed, and I assured her things would be okay. I also routinely checked in with her via text message and offered encouraging words. There came a point when the issue became too much for her, and she no longer wanted to remain in the home. I immediately opened up my home to her. She stayed with me and James. Again, we talked, prayed, ate, and spent time together. She became my daughter—not merely a church member—and I treated her as such. Whatever she needed, I provided it.

> Then the King will say to those on his right, "Come you who are blessed by my Father; take your inheritance the kingdom prepared for you since the creation of the world. For I was hungry and you gave me something to eat, I was thirsty and you gave me something to drink, I was a stranger and you invited me in, I needed clothes and you clothed me, I was sick and you looked after me, I was in

prison and you came to visit me." The King will reply, "Truly I tell you, whatever you did for one of the least of these brothers and sisters of mine, you did for me." (Matthew 25:34–36, 40 NLT)

A couple of months ago, a teenager from my church was narrowing down her high school options. She is very bright, so I suggested a really great school that offers a boarding option for its upper (high school) students. I checked in with her a few weeks ago. She did not apply to the school I recommended. She mentioned being admitted to a different high school but afterward regretted her choice. I was saddened because the school she chose might not provide the rigor she needs or best prepare her for college. I left that conversation wondering what more I could have done. Maybe I should have spoken directly with her family, although no one solicited my advice. I felt badly about the situation.

At a recent church service, a member approached me to ask if I would help her younger brother with his college application process. I leaped at the opportunity, even though he is a couple of years away from attending college. I cannot wait to assist him and am thankful that God has placed this opportunity before me.

We live in and outside of the four walls of a church building. Therefore, ministry and mentoring opportunities will come from inside and outside of church. In God's eyes, our lives are ministry. A former colleague of mine runs a professional development organization for young people between the ages of eighteen to twenty-four. The organization places youth with employers, based on their interests, and helps them navigate the workplace. The young people gather weekly to discuss their experiences and participate in workshops covering specific topics. For many participants, this program is their first experience working professionally. Participants are paired with a mentor to help them navigate the process and keep them motivated. Last winter, my friend contacted me about serving as a mentor for a young lady in her program. I mentioned that folks are watching us. She had informally assessed me during our years of working together and determined that the young lady (Jessica) and I would be a good mentor-mentee match. I agreed to serve.

I was asked to initiate contact with Jessica, attend a program orientation, and spend time with her a couple of times a month. We were to discuss whatever she wanted during our one-on-one time. We have gone out to eat and have seen a movie; I have invited her to my home for a meal, and she has attended my church. We have exercised together, and she and I will go skiing next weekend. Jessica graduated from the professional development program, and I would say my former colleague was accurate. The pairing has been beneficial for us both. Jessica now has a polished resume and knows how to prepare a cover letter. The employer she most desired to work with hired her, and we are now working on the home-buying process. She will become a first-time homebuyer this year. With my son away at college, the opportunity has allowed me to pour energy into someone else instead of watching the paint dry at home.

But I have not always gotten it right. I have not always availed myself of mentoring opportunities when they arose, and I deeply regret it. For instance, I was recently sitting on my sofa when another former colleague contacted me. She knew of a young lady in need of a mentor and asked if I would help. The young lady dropped out of high school and was enrolling in a program that would assist her with reenrolling in high school or obtaining her GED. It was a residential program based outside of the city and required participants to have a mentor to guide them through the process. I called the child's mother to get more details about her, her daughter, and their expectations. I called the program to learn more about their requirements and past successes. This mentoring opportunity was fast-tracked and would require more out of me.

The mother wanted to meet the next day (over a holiday weekend) because the program began the day after that. I had to take my son to college that weekend, and I was not sure I could effectively mentor the young lady. And being super holy—as I sometimes am—instead of being Spirit-led, I needed time to pray and think. I knew I could do it. I knew I was meant to do it. It simply required more effort than I was willing to give without enough notice. This was an opportunity for me to step up my game. I, however, got in the way and decided against mentoring the young lady.

My mind was unsettled for a number of days after making that decision. I wondered if she had found someone else. I wondered how she was faring in the program. I called my colleague to ask whom she had found in my stead to mentor the young lady; she had not found anyone. I called the girl's mother, and her phone was disconnected. I called the program and learned the girl had dropped out after only a few days. She was homesick. I could only wonder if I would have made a difference. Please do not be left with that feeling. Should God provide an opportunity for you to mentor someone and you know within your innermost being it is for you, do it. Souls are waiting. Lives will be changed. Mentor.

Be Still, Be Open

Read and reflect on scriptural texts found in the gospels of Luke and Matthew cited in the devotional above. Answer the questions and complete the exercise provided below.

- What are you presently doing to allow your light to shine in someone else's life?

- Is there more you can and want to do? What would that look like?

- If you are not currently mentoring or pouring into someone, are there opportunities you can seize?

- What attributes do others most admire in you? What skill sets do you possess that others may benefit from?

- Is there a certain group or demographic you feel most compassionate toward?

Exercise: If you are not yet mentoring someone, identify and research a few local organizations this week that assist your preferred demographic. Contact them and volunteer your services.

- Journal your experiences this week.

Lord, I promise _____
_____
_____

Dear God, allow me to serve as Your beacon for others in need. Lord, bring to my remembrance all those who have played an awesome role in my life. I pray for them at this very moment. Bless them, Lord, and meet every need and desire they have. I also ask that You place in my heart someone I may assist. Keep that person, Lord, and help him or her not to faint before You allow our paths to cross. Prepare me and strengthen me for the task. In Jesus's name I pray. Amen.

CHAPTER 8

Learn Something New: Get a Hobby

Sow your seed in the morning, and at evening let your hands not be idle.

—Ecclesiastes 11:6a NIV

A gentleman from church once commented on my son who was about to leave home for college and asked what I would do with myself. I did not know how to respond. Glibly, I said I would live like any other bachelorette: go out, eat out, dine at other people's homes, and so forth. But I truly had not thought about it. What would I do? What are you doing in the meantime?

His question and the time leading up to James's departure made me think. I am a list maker. I thought about and jotted down things I always wanted to try to do.

○ Get my pilot's license
○ Skydive
○ Take piano lessons

○ Take ballroom dance lessons
○ Visit Greece and Rome
○ Learn to play golf

40

I then researched the opportunities to see where and when they were offered in my area and how much they cost. That is the planner in me. Would you know that each of these activities costs too much? Shucks! Based on my finances, I had to think a tad more realistically. It surely is good to have goals, but I needed realistic short-term goals in order to jump-start my new hobby or endeavor.

Exercise became my hobby. If you knew me growing up, you would attest that exercising was not my thing. I equated it with being athletic, and I was not. I did not join any sports club at that age. I was studious, and what did studious high school students do? They joined ROTC. You got it. I was an ROTC girl. Ha! No gym or learning how to swim for me. I swapped suicide drills and pushups for marching, drilling, and shooting rifles.

Shortly before James went away to college, I enrolled in a strength and conditioning class offered at my previous job. A coworker encouraged me to enroll with her. Granted, I tried this working out thing with coworkers before. You know what happened? We went out to eat after work instead of going to the gym. But this time, there was no excuse to dodge going to the gym because the class was in my office building. So my coworker and I went downstairs twice a week and worked out. Oh, my goodness, that man (the instructor) was no joke. It was circuit training. Each participant, regardless of his or her fitness level, spent a minute on every exercise in a rotation for the full forty-minute class. You get that? That's forty exercises. There were squats, weights, lunges, push-ups, sit-ups, burpees, and whatever else you can name. We used resistance bands, exercise balls, and everything in between.

In the beginning, I did not complete as many repetitions in a minute as my classmates. But by the end of my time in the class, I kicked butt and looked like it. Thank God! Surprisingly, I actually liked working out and was saddened when I accepted another job elsewhere. I begged the instructor to continue working with me. Since I was leaving my job, he could not allow me to remain in the class. It also cost too much for me to work with him on my own. I began working from home and gained some weight. *Uh, oh*, I told myself. There was no way I would go from swimsuit cutie to beach cover-up hottie. I researched fitness classes in my area that worked with my schedule and found a twice-weekly boot camp class. From there I began working with a trainer three days a week, and I now work out on my own at least three times a week, incorporating a Zumba class or two.

Alicia, what are you saying? Start somewhere. Make a list of activities you are interested in. Determine which ones fit your budget, schedule them, and hop to it. Time is of the essence. You do not want to look back and wish you had embarked on a hobby. It can be photography. Purchase a camera or use the happy snap one you have and get busy. If your interest is baking, find some awesome recipes or create your own and give treats to friends, coworkers, and neighbors. Get to baking, and bless others with your snacks.

I have revisited some of the hobbies for which I did not initially have the money. Last summer, the golf bug somehow bit me. I really wanted to learn how to play. First things first, though; I needed golf clubs. Purchasing golf clubs and other equipment can be the cost-prohibitive part of golfing. But the financial planner in me started thinking. I like thrift stores and consignment shops. The summer is prime time for yard sales. So I learned about and visited a yard sale in a nice area near my home. Several people within that community came together that day to sell items. *Bingo!* I thought. The likelihood of finding golf clubs among several sellers was good. I arrived first thing that Saturday morning. James will verify that because he was honestly a bit annoyed that I made him go with me. But how can you turn down such an excited mom? I was determined to find a set of golf clubs.

We drove up to the yard sale as the sellers were still arranging their items on the lawn. I saw a lone golf club resting against the concrete walkway. I inquired about the club and was led to the homeowner. She told me that her husband was an avid golfer but was unsure if he would be selling any of his clubs. She, however, introduced me to him. I exuberantly explained my interest in purchasing a set of clubs. He took me inside his home, led me to his basement utility closet, opened the closet door, and revealed four sets of golf clubs. Jackpot! He pulled out his son's set and took me out back to hit. I hit and hit and hit, and eventually the man came back and sold me his son's clubs, golf bag, gloves, and all the golf balls I could handle for fifty dollars. Sold!

I have since stumbled upon a community of golfers in my social circle. Who knew? After that day, I putted with a couple of friends who do not mind giving pointers. I will endeavor to enroll in golf lessons (in between or after completing my LSAT classes) this spring and/or summer. There is a golf course within a mile of my home and another one in the city that offers lessons. I will be there. Where will you be? Join me and tackle a new hobby. Learn something new!

Be Still, Be Open

Read and reflect on Ecclesiastes 11:6. Answer the questions and complete the exercise provided below.

- Are there activities you have always wanted to try?

- Go gangbusters and list them.

Exercise: This week, review your budget and time availability. Prioritize your proposed activity list according to your time and budget constraints. Research local programs and enroll in one. Do it!

- Journal your experiences this week.

Lord, I promise _____

_____

_____

Dear God, I thank You for the gifts of joy and laughter. I ask that You allow me to fully exude both of them. Place opportunities before me that will both lighten my heart and endear me to new endeavors. Bless those I encounter and join in this new activity. And prepare the environment for my arrival. Allow me to continue to carry You wherever I go. Allow my lifestyle and relationship with You to bless someone else. Create an opportunity for a soul to be ministered to and saved as a result of this new door, which You are opening. In Jesus's name I pray. Amen.

CHAPTER 9

Pay Off Your Debt

Blessed are those who find wisdom, those who gain understanding, for she is more profitable than silver and yields better returns that gold. She is more precious than rubies; nothing you desire can compare with her. Long life is in her right hand.
—Proverbs 3:13–16a NIV

I cannot trace a single historical event that would explain how or when I became a saver. I can only share bits and pieces that probably all add up to a full portrait. I remember having a LaSalle Bank passbook savings account as a child. My grandfather would take me to a local branch to make deposits whenever I scored a fat check or a loaded birthday card. He was also a saver. I went to the bank with him frequently. Visiting the bank was one of his usual weekend errands.

I remember lending money to one of my mother's boyfriends. Man, I made so much money off of him. He would borrow twenty dollars from me one week on the condition that he paid me forty dollars the next week. Sweet! I was raking in the cash.

My first job was working as a cashier at Montgomery Ward. Remember that store? Like Woolworth's, it no longer exists. I worked in the electronics department, which meant I sold beepers and telephones. Do you remember pagers? Chronicling my life against the economic and technological changes of the last twenty years is making me feel old.

After a short stint at Montgomery Ward, I worked as a receptionist at a local bank. One of my high school classmates worked there and told me the bank was hiring. We held the same position but worked different shifts. That job was cool. It was an old-school type of bank that gave employees watches when they retired and turkeys for Thanksgiving dinner. I was sixteen years old and bringing home a turkey for Thanksgiving. Ha! I brought home the bacon early in life. I opened my first checking account and saved all my paychecks while working at the bank.

I do not recall anyone ever sitting me down to say debt was bad. I think I just knew it. I grew up in a time when folks did not use credit cards like cash. You either had the money or you did not. So that is the school of thought I came from. It is default discipline because one would either pay for something or save for it. Those were and still ought to be our only two options. And that is what I do. I do not want to be like my mother's former boyfriend who paid crazy interest on money because he could not wait for what he wanted. Instant gratification—at the risk of going broke—is overrated. What say you? Are you financially disciplined? Do you allow impulsive and temporal desires for *stuff* to overtake you? If so, please stop being enslaved by your desires, and ask God for wisdom and self-control. He is a rewarder of those who diligently seek Him (Hebrews 11:6).

I was thrown off course a bit, however, when I went away to college. I had a couple of department store credit cards. I quickly paid off those credit card bills and closed the accounts. For all the young people reading this book, never close your credit card accounts. Better still, do not get credit cards. Closing your credit cards puts a ding on your credit report and lowers your credit score. This mistake haunts you for seven years—until the history is dropped from your credit report. Just cut up the credit cards, pay off the debt, and never use the account again. If you think about it, this instruction is similar to what Jesus told the woman caught in adultery (John 8:1–11). Her accusers wanted her stoned, but they backed off after realizing they were not without sin. When she was left alone with Him, Jesus told her that He did not condemn her. He instructed her to go and leave her life of sin. So go and leave those credit cards behind.

I mortgaged a condominium at age twenty-five by using Washington, DC's first-time homebuyer program. I received public funds to assist with my closing costs in exchange for a five-year deferred $10,000 loan. After routinely receiving my monthly bill to repay the loan, the arrangement suddenly did not make sense to me. Why did I agree to pay interest on a nineteen-dollar-a-month payment when I could just pay more monthly and completely eliminate the debt sooner? I did not like the idea of spreading out that $10,000 payment over a number of years. I just so happened to stumble upon and take a Dave Ramsey financial management class. The class took place once a night over several weeks and was well worth it. When I began his class, I was paying the requested monthly installments on my $10,000 loan. At that rate I would be paying that debt (for what seemed like) forever, just like my mortgage payment. Shortly into his class, I took money from my savings account and killed that debt. All I had left was my student loans (outside of my mortgages). I was about to snowball the rest of my debt. Snowballing is when you pile up as much cash as possible to knock out one debt and then apply that same cash—plus what is freed up by paying down the first debt—to your next debt.

My student loan came due more than ten years after I graduated from college. For some reason, the US Department of Education was slow to collect my $28,000 student loan debt. My other college friends began paying their loans off almost immediately after college. At first, I paid the minimum amount required, as requested. But after doing the math and realizing that I would be paying that amount for thirty years, I decided to snowball that loan payment. I am about four years into paying off my student loans. I will make my final payment this season and am already devising a plan to kill my condo mortgage in five years. If God be for me, who can be against me?!

Do you have a debt repayment plan? If so, when was the last time you reviewed it? Is it time for it to be revised? Start by tracking your spending for at least two months; reviewing past bank statements is a quick way to do this. Place your expenditures into categories such as savings, housing, transportation, utilities, clothing, recreation, and so forth; review where your money is going. For some people, this is an eye-opening exercise; for others, it is a matter of finally facing their giants. Do this and give God those things and habits you idolize and value too highly. Lay those habits and idols at the Lord's feet. Seek Him for direction and strength, and make cuts to your spending plan in order to find savings. The Lord is good to those who seek Him. He may direct you to cut that phone bill, cancel your cable television service, and subscribe to Netflix. Cook more, and begin taking your lunch to work more often. Take public transportation or carpool instead of commuting solo. Shop at consignment or resale stores. You will not be the first to heed His advice. I do and have done each of these things.

After you have made your cuts, put your new spending plan on paper before God and stick to it (Psalm 119:5). I liken this transformative process to Jesus's work on the cross. He was crucified, His body placed before God, and His words inked on paper for us to follow. Jesus paid our debts so that we could have life. Pay off your debts as preparation for the next phase of life God has for you. The ability to successfully care for your promise depends on it.

Be Still, Be Open

Read and reflect on Proverbs 3. Answer the questions and complete the exercise provided below.

- Would you categorize yourself as a spender, saver, free spirit, or miser?

- What attributes do you have or display leading you to making this assessment?

- In what ways could you tighten or loosen (for you misers out there) your financial belt?

- Do you have an up-to-date budget or spending plan (for those who do not like the "B" word)?

Exercise: If your budget needs updating (or should you need to create one), identify someone in your circle you deem financially prudent and contact him or her for assistance and tips. If you are not comfortable with this arrangement, research Christian-based financial management courses like the one discussed in the devotion above. Register with one this week. If you're a financial management whiz, ask God to place someone before you to assist.

- Journal your experiences this week.

Lord, I promise _____

_____

_____

Dear God, thank You for entrusting me with Your wealth. Renew my mind so I may be a better steward over what You have given me. Help me to not be the borrower, Lord, but to serve as the lender. Allow me to realize opportunities You create to grow my financial abilities or to impart my abilities to someone else. I thank You in advance for increased favor and guidance. In Jesus's name I pray. Amen.

CHAPTER 10

Repair and Strengthen Relationships

For if you forgive those who sin against you, your Heavenly Father will also forgive you. But if you refuse to forgive others, your Father will not forgive your sins.

—Matthew 6:14–15 NLT

My parents got married at age twenty-one. They came from married households, but my grandparents' relationships had dissolved by the time I was born. In my mother's case, her parents separated and lived apart. In my father's case, his parents divorced. My entire immediate family lived in the city. My parents, however, moved to a white suburb when I was a toddler. They had good jobs. My mother worked for Illinois Bell (now AT&T), and my father worked in law enforcement for the county sheriff. My youngest memories are of us living in the suburbs. I had my own room with a record player and a Raggedy Ann doll, among other things. I loved to read (or be read to), and I loved McDonald's filet of fish sandwiches. My aunt used to tease my mother about my being a McDonald's kid. I remember playing Atari with my father and him teaching me how to count money, i.e., the difference between each coin type and its respective value. I believe I now have to wear glasses (I prefer contact lenses) from watching TV too close to the screen with my dad. Life was good.

We moved back to the city after my paternal grandfather died. I was about four years old. I remember us living with my paternal grandmother. I also remember the night my mother and I left. I shared a room with my eldest aunt, who had the thickest Jamaican accent imaginable. I believe I was asleep in my room when my mother awakened me. There was screaming, and my maternal grandfather (Gran) was outside waiting for us. My mother and I moved in with Gran. My parents divorced, and my mother and I stayed with Gran until I was in junior high school.

My mother left my father that night after he tried to kill her. He was on top of her while high on cocaine. He tried to suffocate my mother. She somehow made it out from under him, got me, and left. Over the next thirteen years, I visited my father at my grandmother's house. That is where he lived. My grandmother was the best. She was and is a strong, natural Jamaican beauty. She taught me how to be a lady. I learned from her everything pertaining to grooming myself, how to properly wear undergarments, how to behave, and how to identify and wear clothing that fit my body type. She also taught me how to navigate the bus system. We took the bus everywhere. I enjoyed my time with my grandmother. She took care of me when I visited my father. I do not recall spending that much time with him during those visits. He lived his life, which did not really include me. Yes, he taught me my times tables, and we occasionally watched TV together. But he spent much of his time getting high and chasing women.

My mother raised me, and I loved her. She worked for the city. We never lacked—not in my eyes. As mentioned earlier, I worked for a bank while in high school and had my first checking account at age sixteen. The bank directly deposited my paychecks, and I saved them. I was saving to buy a computer for college. After some time, I discovered that money was missing from my account. My checking account statement detailed random ten- and twenty-dollar withdrawals. I was confused. I remember talking about it with my aunt, my father's sister. She said it was time to reveal something with me. She shared that my mother was a drug abuser and might have taken the money. This is hard to write.

I confronted my mother, and she admitted to taking the money. I immediately put her on a repayment plan. Now that her secret was out, my mother did not try to hide her addiction. She would go out at random times. I would argue with her about it, and our relationship deteriorated. I went away to college not long after learning of her drug habit.

College was cool. I joined the campus gospel choir, excelled in my studies, and remained focused. Upon graduating, I applied to and was admitted to graduate school at home in Chicago. They gave me a free ride, and on I rode!

My mother (and father, surprisingly) came to my college graduation. She was so thin. It was evident that her addiction had worsened. She wanted me to move in with her when I returned home. I really did not want to live with her; I wanted to live with Gran but did not want to hurt her feelings. Grudgingly, I moved in with my mother and started grad school. School was cool. Home was not. Mom became increasingly frail; she was literally a walking skeleton. I remember when one of my best friends visited our home, saw my mother, and asked me if she was okay. She knew of my mother's condition. It was not something I hid.

By that time, my mother had gone all out. She came home all hours of the night. She ditched work and neglected to pay our bills, which became overdue. Our landlord approached me about the rent because we were behind in payments. I contacted my mother's employer to learn about her benefits plan. Her insurance offered counseling and treatment for substance abusers. I researched a few places and presented my mother with the options. She did not go, and her destructive behavior continued. It was hard to focus on my studies. I moved out, completed my final year of grad school, and moved to Washington, DC.

I cannot really recall what birthed it or how it came about (maybe it is because things were rocky with my mother), but at that time, I greatly desired a real relationship with my father. I forgave him. So I called him to tell him just that. I knew he was not in a space to hear it, but I wanted to put it out there. I had the talk. I shared with him that I really wanted us to get to know each other and to communicate regularly. A weight was lifted. I now just had to wait for him to come around, and that was okay.

My mother and I remained close, but admittedly, something was missing on my end. I was privately guarded with her. I knew people who called their parents multiple times a day or who visited their parents several times a year. I did not do that. Not to say they were right and I was not. I just did not call or visit my mother that often. We talked, we shared, but I withheld parts of myself from her. She knew it, but I did not. I did not realize it. It was my new normal.

My father had bypass surgery a few years ago. Shortly afterward, Gran died. James and I went home for the home-going service. We stayed in Chicago longer than we normally do, since I planned and paid for the home-going service. My family went out to eat after the service. While having dinner, my mother asked me if my father had a stroke. I said that I did not know. She noticed that his walk and speech was slower than she remembered. I had not noticed anything until she pointed it out. I share this because it was during this time, when my father's health began failing him, that he forged a real relationship with me.

God slowed my father down. My father began calling me. When we talked, he would actually ask how I was doing. That was major. All my life, everything had always been about him. He had always been the focal point of our conversations. He always talked about his plans and what he was doing. But he changed. Our conversations changed. He wanted to know me.

Last summer, one of my pastors taught a Bible study lesson on love. We read 1 Corinthians 13 for homework. She asked us to dissect and write a summary on the chapter. I did the assignment but did not realize how powerful it would be for me. Here is a portion of what I wrote:

> The lack of love, either in fully receiving, giving, or expressing it, hinders us from getting, becoming, and being God's best.
>
> As part of an earlier Bible study, I discussed the difference between surviving and thriving. As a reminder, surviving is to remain alive—after someone's death—or to continue to exist. Remember Charlie Brown's Christmas tree? It was surviving. I believe that is what happens when we exist without tapping into God's gift of love by fully having, receiving, giving, or expressing it as noted in 1 Corinthians 13:1–3. In life and in ministry, we can have all the knowledge and wealth known to man. We can have all the faith to move mountains, but without love our knowledge, wealth and faith is useless. We are simply ineffective hoarders in that these gifts do not benefit our fellow brethren. It only benefits us as we merely survive.
>
> Similar to the Scripture, faith without works is dead. I believe gifts without love are dead. First Corinthians 13:8 reads, "But where there are prophecies, they will cease; where there are tongues, they will be stilled; where there is knowledge, it will pass away" (NIV).

Without love, our gifts and ability to give life dies. Going back to the difference between surviving and thriving, if we were to thrive in life—meaning, to grow vigorously or to progress toward or realize a goal and/or God's best in our lives and in our walk—our love would be *felt*. We would be moving mountains for others, speaking life into them, and meeting the needs of those around us. Doing greater works. Our gifts, wealth, and lives would be made perfect through love.

For we know in part and we prophesy in part, but when perfection comes, the imperfect disappears.
—1 Corinthians 13:9–10 NIV

Love is the glue that binds us, completes us, and perfects us and our gifts. Having, receiving, sharing, and expressing love—with our gifts and lives—helps us receive and become God's best. Without it, we are merely ineffective clanging cymbals, stilled tongues, and unfulfilled prophecies.

After completing this assignment and really allowing the Word to minister to me, I realized the error of my ways. I needed to repair another relationship. I called my mother. I shared that we had grown distant because of her addiction. I told her that I loved her and desired her to be clean. I told her that God loved her and desired to heal whatever issues birthed and enabled her addiction. I forgave her. And I told her that she was worthy of His restoration and that she could fully be made whole. I told her that she was strong enough to beat her addiction—with God's help. She cried as she listened. It was a transformative discussion. I closed by telling her that I loved her.

Now my mother is clean. While her struggle is not easy, her relationship with Christ is stronger. She attends church regularly.

She prays more, and she fasted for the first time a week or so ago. My mother fasted, y'all! Praise God! That is major. I praise God and am proud of her. To Him be all the glory and honor. I should also add that our relationship is better. In fact, my mother and I are vacationing together this fall. We are going to Montego Bay, Jamaica with my father's family. This is huge. Outside of family trips to Kentucky as a child, we have never vacationed together. She has also never traveled abroad. I offered to cover her trip if she purchased her passport. Do you know that she went to city hall for a new birth certificate, to CVS for passport photos, and to the post office for her passport application that same week? If you knew my mother before that call last summer, you would be shouting! Again, I praise God and I look forward to His continued movement in her life and in our relationship.

My meantime is preparation for the husband God will grace me with. What is yours? I cannot go into a lifelong committed relationship of God's design with emotional pain and baggage. I have had to mend relationships. What about you? Are there relationships you can and need to repair? God truly will not bless mess. Please take the necessary steps to forgive, call, and talk it out with whomever God lays on your heart. Life is not promised, nor is eternal life guaranteed without repentance from sin. Open yourself up to being fully healed. Repair relationships in your meantime while you still have the time. Your next step forward greatly depends on it.

Be Still, Be Open

Read and reflect on Matthew 6:14–15 and 1 Corinthians 13. Answer the questions and complete the exercise provided below.

- Are there relationships you can strengthen and improve? If so, list them here.

- What has stopped you from doing so up until now?

- Do you have new understanding of forgiveness and love? How are they freeing you?

- Whom must you contact and/or what must you face this week to move forward?

Exercise: If the person you must forgive or contact is deceased, forgive him or her aloud in prayer and release yourself from the weight you have been carrying. If you own objects that remind you of estranged relationships and weighty feelings, take them outside, pray over them aloud, and throw them away. If you need to face yourself, write down some remarks to yourself, and read them aloud in a mirror while looking at yourself.

- Journal your experiences this week.

Lord, I promise _____
_____
_____

Dear God, thank You for not forgetting about me and creating an opportunity for me to be lighter in You. Lord, I forgive myself for holding on to lack of forgiveness and for not fully loving others and myself the way You love. I ask that You reveal more of Your loving nature to me. Grant me opportunities to display greater love and compassion to others. According to Your will, fully heal and restore my sore relationships. Anoint me with Your salve, and seal up wounds I may have carried with me. Thank You, Lord. In Jesus's name I pray. Amen.

CHAPTER 11

Dump Some Stuff

Therefore, since we are surrounded by such a great
cloud of witnesses, let us throw off everything that
hinders and the sin that so easily entangles, and let
us run with perseverance the race marked out for us.
—Hebrews 12:1 NIV

We have arrived at the topic most folks cannot wait to dive into.
It is common when it comes to single women. Everyone wants to
know about our love lives. "Are you seeing anyone? Who are you
seeing? Tell me about him." This is how a typical conversation goes
between a single woman and anyone she speaks to. Those are the
polite questions.

Sometimes we are sucker-punched with the two big questions:
When are you getting married, and when will you make me a
grandparent? These come when and after we reach thirty years of
age. We are typically asked these questions when visiting family,
talking on the phone with family, walking past a family member,
sneezing around family, or reaching for the remote control. You get
the picture. That is probably another reason why I live out of state.
(I am just kidding.)

I explained the *who* of my relationship history in an earlier chapter. Now it is time to delve more into *why* through an illustrative example. I have had to dump some things in the process of becoming the helpmate God requires me to be. The spirits and behaviors I have dumped include moving out of God's timing, not trusting God, fear of failure, and pride. What do you need to dump?

Some time ago, I was reading the Bible in a room at church before my youth Sunday school class arrived. While reading, I had a vision. I was standing beside a young man I knew. It was as if we were about to exchange wedding vows. Once the vision ended, I said something to the effect of, "Uh … Jesus, that cannot be."

In real life, it was clear this young man was interested in me. We had been friends for years. People who knew us suggested I date him. He was younger than I, so I had reservations about his age and his level of maturity. But, if I were honest with myself, I did find him attractive, we did have chemistry, and I was interested in him. So I immediately caught myself after my "uh … Jesus" moment and said, "Okay, God, if this is what You are suggesting, I will trust You."

Not too long after having the vision, I asked someone who felt the young man and I should date to encourage him to pursue me. And pursue he did. We creatively dated for a short while because he was not fully employed and did not have an income. I was okay with this circumstance because I had known him and his family for years. I knew he would soon land a good position. He, however, was not so sure and was not yet ready to become serious. His not being ready soon manifested itself. Admittedly, we had sex, and he got scared after one occasion due to his premature performance and fear that I might become pregnant. He asked me what to do. I said that he would not like my answer but all we could do was wait. After that day, he began avoiding me. (Sex outside of marriage is a sin in the eyes of God, and I have repented for this behavior).

I never in my life had to take a pregnancy test, and now I had to take one on my own. Remember: he left, so I took the test and text messaged him a picture of the results, since he would not communicate with me any other way.

What did I learn? I should not have moved outside of God's timing. God would have created the appointed time for this young man to pursue me without my help. I should have taken my own advice about waiting.

A year and a half passed. During that period, we did not communicate much with one another. It was not my choice, although I was quite hurt. But he no longer felt comfortable around me. We resumed communication at some point, and I could sense his continued interest in me. I also had dreams during this time about him suggesting that our relationship was not over. I discerned that he was working up the courage to pursue me once more. And he did.

We met one evening and talked about what occurred the first time around—our previous offenses and all. Afterward, he mentioned an interest in seeing where things could go between us. I said okay, and we began dating again. It was better the second time around. He was employed, which I knew put him at ease. He was more mature in that I could see him taking things I said to heart. He also began to open up and be more vulnerable. We were clicking.

I, however, was not as open. I definitely felt a good "this is it" and a knowing when were we together, like an electrical energy. I was more open with him than I had been with anyone else in *years*. I felt I could be my true self with him without any reservations. But I did not communicate some of my innermost feelings or concerns to him. I was afraid that if I did, he would leave.

One of my concerns was about being sexually intimate. I had been celibate for close to seven years before we first had sex together. I was afraid to share my desire for us to wait. I was afraid he would leave if I were not intimate with him. Certain things he did or did not do also concerned me. Arriving late for dates was one of them. I do not like wondering if a man will show up. Also, he would not apologize for things, no matter how trivial. This all triggered memories of my father. When I was younger, my father would make arrangements to take me places or to come and get me and not show up. And I would wait for him. Waiting on this young man to arrive after we made plans brought back those anxieties.

My father had been unapologetic about his actions. This young man's actions also brought that memory back to me. Therefore, when it came to expressing how I felt, I lost my voice and failed to communicate—just as I had done years before with my dad after he hurt or disappointed me. Then my mother wondered why I would not tell my father how I felt. I was afraid he would leave or not show up. That is exactly how I felt about opening up to the young man I was dating. I also began to think of reasons why our relationship would not work and of all the ways I might eventually be hurt. So I ended it before he could leave.

I did not trust God to deliver me into a loving relationship of His design. I could not see it panning out, because I was afraid of it failing—the way my parents' marriage and my relationship with my parents had failed. I could see he was hurt that I had ended our relationship. I knew he cared for me and wanted to continue seeing me. I just could not do it, because I was scared of the relationship failing. I was scared of being hurt, and I did not trust God.

Other people could sense my feelings and would comment to me that I was in love with him. I was, but I would not allow myself to acknowledge how I truly felt about him. And it was hard seeing him all the time while trying to get over him. I tried so hard to deny my feelings for him, but they remained. Over the next several months, I continued having dreams about him. God showed me my disobedience and His desire that I reconnect with the young man. I simply would not do it. I was Jonah. I knew it, and God told me so. But unlike Jonah, I did not ultimately fulfill my God-given assignment.

Later, I had a dream. It was about me running into a house to choose the best room before anyone else arrived. I found a room that I liked but wanted to see if there were other rooms I liked better. So I went looking at other rooms. When I determined that my first room was the best, I went back to it to discover that it was occupied, and the new occupant would not let me have it. God was speaking.

A little later, the young man began seeing someone else. It really did not bother me, or so I thought. But oh, boy, pride ballooned out of nowhere. *She's not me! She can't do x, y and z like I can!* That is what I told myself and how I justified not caring. I was a hot mess and proud beyond measure. Periodically, he would still reach out to me via text. God is something else. I would honestly be thinking about him, and he would text me. I, however, would ignore his text messages, all the while knowing I wanted to be with him. I was scared. I was also trying to move on and allow him to do the same.

One day, I decided to contact him. I finally had enough of not being able to get him off my mind. But before I called him, something told me to visit Facebook. I hardly ever visited Facebook. I went to his page, and there was a photo of him with the young lady he was seeing. He was in love. I could see it in his eyes. I then saw his status and it read *engaged*. I became sick instantly, and I ran to the bathroom to vomit.

I saw him the next day. I put on my big-girl panties and faced him. I congratulated him on his engagement and shared that I wished him the best. I was honest. I wanted him to be happy.

My faith was tested and strengthened as a result of that relationship. In the Bible, Jacob wrestled with God and was named *Israel*. In real life, I wrestled with my inner me and my different strongholds and am now humble. I had time to work through that season of my life. Those months of having to regularly see him, while enduring his engagement, blessed me. It did not feel like a blessing, but God held up a mirror to my face and the Holy Spirit dug up a lot of stuff (old wine) within me. It took a lot of crying, reading and standing on specific Scripture, praying, worshipping, fasting, travailing, speaking with trusted confidantes, reconciling other relationships, and forgiving myself in order to heal and move on. I am *over* moving out of God's timing, not trusting God, fearing failure, and letting pride obstruct me. I thank God!

God is now speaking to me again about marriage. It is His promise to me. I am encouraged and thankful for second chances. In the meantime, I have taken time to learn more about God's design for marriage. I am allowing His Word to teach and heal me. Whenever doubt tries to creep in (because of how much time has passed or because of other things), God gives me His aroma, a whiff of His promise. He will remind me of His word or send someone to speak into my life specifically about His promise. I have encountered a prophetess and other ministers of the gospel who have shared that I will soon be married and who also gave me instructions. I have stepped out on faith and purchased a wedding gown—husband unseen—because I was instructed to do so. I continue to actively wait on His promise by preparing myself through the opportunities and assignments He gives me.

Much of this in the meantime preparation has been shared with you in earlier chapters. I am dancing, teaching, learning new things, endeavoring to go back to school, dumping debt, repairing relationships, writing a book, and being receptive to whatever else God speaks as He molds me into the optimal wife for the man He has for me. I know it all will be well worth it. I hope and pray you will also seek and heed God's instruction for your meantime activities. Your meantime has begun. Do what is required to prepare yourself to receive His promise.

Be Still, Be Open

Read and reflect on Hebrews 12:1. Answer the questions and fulfill the requests made below.

- What baggage must you dump before you can move forward in God's promise?

- Why have you held on to this weight? Add this *why* to your dump list.

- How is your baggage negatively impacting you and your relationships?

- Dump each *bag* aloud to God in prayer.

- Journal your experiences this week.

Lord, I promise _____

_____

_____

Dear God, I thank You for loving me and wanting me to be made whole. I accept Your love and declare to love myself more. Lord, show me how You so lovingly see me, so I may grow to see myself the same way. Take from me all the hurt, pain, grief, and other ungodly spirits I have held on to. Grant me Your peace. Heal my heart and renew my mind. Close all doors that need to be closed in order to forever seal this chapter of my life. And be with me as I walk through the new doors You have opened before me. I bless Your holy name. In Jesus's name I pray. Amen.

CHAPTER 12

Write a Book

You were running a good race. Who cut in on you
to keep you from obeying the truth? That kind of
persuasion does not come from the one who calls you.
—Galatians 5:7–8 NIV

I must admit that I have always wanted to write a book. Wanting
to do something and actually doing it, however, are two dissimilar
things. They each require something different. We all fantasize,
dream, and aspire to do things. Why not? Wishing comes easily. All
it takes is a wandering mind and a desire. We say, I would love to x,
y, and z. And poof! We have a dream. But how many of us actually
act on what we ponder, hope, and dream about? Action. That is both
the key difference and the key ingredient. We must act. But what
holds us back? What trips us up? What stops us? Now that I have
dumped fear and lack of faith, I simply need a little push.

Last fall, I attended a prayer conference in Richmond, Virginia.
The prophetess I mentioned in an earlier chapter was one of the
featured ministers. I could not wait to attend. I knew God would
speak a timely word, and I was ready to receive it. In fact, James
was game as well, which was extraordinary because he does not

like attending conferences. I was also wonderfully surprised when a confidante and fellow minister agreed to attend and ride down with me and James. Her agreeing to attend confirmed for me that God was up to something.

Early that Saturday morning, we left for Richmond from my home. The drive was good. We were cruising down I-95. James was in the backseat grooving to the music playing through his headphones. And my "sister" and I were up front enjoying a really great conversation when suddenly I had to brake, switch lanes to the shoulder, and drive a few car lengths before merging back into traffic. The car in front of us put on its brakes without warning. Whew! That was scary, but we all said a "Thank you, Jesus" and continued toward Richmond.

A half hour or so passed, and we were nearing our highway exit. As I tried slowing down to approach and merge onto the exit, I noticed that my brakes were not working. They must have gone out after that earlier, close-call collision. I did not have a clue, because I had not needed to brake until we arrived at our exit. I did not let my passengers know that my brakes had failed; I simply pressed the brake pedal all the way to the floor, prayed inwardly, and drove my car like it was on rails around that curved exit. I know they must have thought I was crazy because of how fast we were going. All I could think about was finding somewhere to pull over.

Once we got off of the highway, one turn led to the next and we were pulling into the conference center site adjacent to the highway exit. Can you say hallelujah? We did. Praise God from whom all blessings flow! Needless to say, my car was done for after we miraculously arrived. I must have been in shock and had not fully processed what just happened, because I did not call for a tow. We simply headed straight into the hotel for church service.

If you have not guessed by now, I am a bit of a nerd. Wherever I go, I usually sit near the front. So when we found the room where the service was to be held, I made myself comfortable near the front. When the service started, there were opening remarks, Scripture reading, prayer, and a dance. The prophetess then began ministering. After her Spirit-filled remarks, the Holy Spirit led her to minister directly to individuals. As she was prophesying to the person next to me, I began writing a key piece of her message that stood out to me. I wanted to jot it down and share it with the woman she was speaking to afterward. Right then, unexpectedly, the prophetess turned to me and shared a four-minute prophecy with me (I have the DVD). The first thing God said to me was, "So you are a scribe. So I anoint you to write. You are my writer. The book is in you." He proceeded to share a host of other things with me through her. It was a rich experience.

After the service, everyone was full. There was not much to say. We were stuck in awe trying to absorb all that God had shared with us. We walked over to another building for lunch and ate. At that point, I must have calmed down and come to myself. It was not until after lunch that I realized I needed to call my insurance company to report what had occurred and schedule a tow truck to come and get my car. When the tow truck driver arrived, he was amazed that we had made it to the hotel safely. The brake line on my car was shot, and the brakes were verifiably dead. He did not know how we made it from the highway to the hotel or how I managed to back into a parking space. It was all God. It was purposed for us—His precious cargo—to attend that conference and receive His word.

God said so much to me through the prophetess that I admittedly did not think much about writing a book after that day. When I had thought about and expressed an interest in writing a book in the past, I had said I would leave it to God. He would surely give me who, what, when, where, and why. Until then, I did not have a clue about what to write. So after the prayer conference, I went back home to Washington, DC and continued my daily routine while waiting on the Lord to manifest what He released in His time. I left the book and everything else up to Him. I would need a push.

About three months later, a sister in Christ, whom I had recently gotten to know, invited me out to lunch. She and I had previously tried for some time to connect in person, but our schedules kept conflicting. Fortunately, this Friday afternoon proved different. Before leaving my house to meet her, I prayed. I asked God to bless our fellowship together. I asked that He make our time together purposeful, that He be in our midst, that He do all the speaking, and that we have a good time. When I arrived to meet her at the restaurant, she shared that her sister would be joining us. I said okay, and we chatted and ordered our food until her sister arrived.

Our fellowship was good. We had a great time talking about everything imaginable and sharing things about ourselves. The sister who arrived late said that she was writing her tenth book. It was a collection of chapters written by various women sharing their individual testimonies in order to empower other women. She asked if I would write a chapter in her book. I mentioned that I could not think of anything serious that I had been delivered from. I had not been battered, drug dependent, molested, or raped. So I did not think I had much to say. Instead, I provided her with the names of two other ladies I knew who had powerful testimonies. We continued our talk, paid our bill, and left. It was a good time.

After arriving home, I wondered if I had just missed God. Was He offering me the chance to contribute to someone's book? Did I say no to an opportunity that was meant for me? I contacted a confidante of mine and asked her opinion, and of course she said it was meant for me to do. I, however, could not fathom what I could possibly share. What had I been delivered from? She offered me two examples, from having known me, of what I could share. I thought it over for a few days, began writing, and finished the chapter in one sitting. I sent it to my confidante to read. She liked it. I tweaked it a bit more and sent it on to the young woman for her book. I needed a push.

A couple of months later, I attended a leadership class at my church, which was geared toward current ministers. For the session, my pastor invited a fellow pastor to speak. As part of his remarks, the guest pastor spoke about a season called *the meantime.* He mentioned that many Christians struggle during this period of time while they await the manifestation of God's promise—whatever that promise might be for them. He said there was a void in the body of Christ because of a lack of assistance for people in this season of life. He also said there was a lack of information and resources to help Christians sustain and operate in the meantime. That message and term *in the meantime* struck me and stayed with me. It really made sense and rang true for me and for other ladies in the class. It described where we are. We are waiting, but not many of us know how to wait or what to do in the meantime.

Did not the prophetess say that the book was in me? God was working that out because I still had not thought much about it. I needed a push. Four weeks later, I was in my car, about to head home from an event, when a friend from college called me on my cell phone. We had routinely tried to keep in touch, but I had not spoken with her in a while. It was good to hear from her. Amazingly, she began the conversation by declaring that I needed to write a devotional. She said she was thinking about me and the season I am presently in when it came to her that I ought to write a book. What did she know about the season I was in? I broke out in uncontrollable laughter and simultaneously teared up. God is something. I knew He was speaking to me.

I knew my friend was puzzled by my laughing response, so I revealed that she was not the first person to share this suggestion with me. My friend is a professional counselor, so she immediately wanted to identify and work through any obstacles hindering my writing a book. Fortunately, she is good at what she does and has known me long enough that she did not need to brainstorm about my reluctance.

She said, "Alicia, you are your own obstacle. You are in a season of waiting that lends itself to opportunities. You put self-imposed limits on yourself."

God was speaking. I then shared that I did not know what to write about. My encouraging friend ran through a list of potential topics based on her knowledge of my gifts. I typed them all down in my phone as she spoke and promised that I would pray and ask God for further direction. I needed a push.

Three days after the conversation, I interviewed for a job before a panel of three gentlemen. One of the men was extremely quiet and had not asked a single question. When it was time for me to ask questions of the panel, I engaged the quiet gentleman and asked if he had any questions for me. He replied, "You should write a book. You have a lot of different experiences."

I blinked and smiled. I was taken aback. I responded by sharing that I had recently written a chapter for someone else's book. He told me to write one page a day for my own book. I was amazed by this interaction. He pushed me and I began writing that day.

Be Still, Be Open

Read and reflect on Galatians 5:7–8. Answer the questions and fulfill the requests made below.

- How does this Scripture apply to you? What feelings does it bring up for you?

- What race and/or task has God asked you to complete that you have yet to accomplish?

- What is stopping you from completing the task?

- Is there an action or series of actions needed to complete the task? List them.

- What will you do this week to move forward?

- Journal your experiences this week.

Lord, I promise _____

_____

_____

Dear God, I thank You for new mercies each day and ask that You forgive me for not making haste to accomplish the plans You have for me. Father, strengthen my faith, give me wisdom, arm me with Your power, help me to know Your voice, show me Your will, and instruct me on how to proceed. I thank You in advance for your awesome provision. Keep me encouraged and allow me to receive those You send to help me. I bless You and thank You for the opportunity to grow in You. In Jesus's name I pray. Amen.

CHAPTER 13

Crush the Enemy

I have found David my servant; with my sacred oil
I have anointed him. My hand will sustain him;
surely my arm will strengthen him. The enemy
will not get the better of him; the wicked will not
oppress him. I will crush his foes before him and
strike down his adversaries. My faithful love will
be with him, and through my name his horn will
be exalted.

—Psalm 89:20–24 NIV

Have you noticed that when things are good and steady in your life,
conflict suddenly comes to knock you out? We believers occasionally
forget, although Jesus died for our sins and promised us eternal life
after we accept salvation, that our lives will surely have their share
of trials and tribulations. As many of us can attest, being laid off,
foreclosed on, widowed, walked out on, or gossiped about does
not feel good. Those of us who read and study the Word of God
sometimes overlook the line that reads, "Indeed we suffer with Him,
that we may also be glorified together" (Romans 8:17 NKJV). I
certainly do not recall seeing Jesus in the flesh suffering beside me

years ago when I was terminated from a previous job. But why not shift our collective perspective from that of a forlorn victim to one of a dearly-loved child?

We are not aware of the constant attacks and assassination attempts the Enemy daily makes on our lives. We are relieved when a careless driver looks up and sees us in the crosswalk moments before what could have been an accident. But I can only fathom how active and embattled the angels assigned to protect us are each day. The small near misses we are allowed to experience pale in comparison. I honestly do not want to know the details of each near-death experience I have unknowingly been rescued from. We wake up each day with new mercies (Lamentations 3:22–23). God's arm of protection constantly covers and shields us. His promises surround us.

The trials that come and sometimes rock us to our cores are actually faith-building and character-refining opportunities meant to lead us into promise. I am reminded of Joseph, whose life is recounted in the book of Genesis, chapters thirty-seven through fifty. Joseph was loved and doted on by his father. The Lord revealed himself to Joseph while he was a teenager. God showed him that he would be great and play a mighty role in His plan. At the same time, however, Joseph's brothers hated him, plotted to kill him, sold him into slavery, and abandoned him. Large purpose (promise) often comes after enduring Hades on earth.

But God was with Joseph, just as He is with you. In his Hades-like situation, Joseph was still favored by God and, accordingly, was purchased by one of Pharoah's officials. The official even realized that God was with Joseph and because of that appointed him as steward over everything he owned. Life was good for Joseph, and yet another life challenge came. He was lied about and placed in prison. But God remained faithful to Joseph and the promise He made for his life. Egypt's prison warden elevated Joseph because of his relationship with God. The warden appointed Joseph over all of the prison's affairs. Who else but God will make your prison your paradise?

I was just faced with a Joseph-type situation. But God is good! Exactly two weeks ago, I was laid off from my job. The day before, God revealed to me that it was going to happen. I woke up the next morning, logged into work, submitted my final invoices, typed my goodbye email, and waited for the phone call. My supervisor called me; I answered the phone in my usual upbeat, joy-filled manner. He was apologetic and saddened to share the news with me. I was fine. I cheerfully thanked him and wished him an awesome day. After hanging up, I pressed "send" on the email I had prepared, logged out, and ended my work day. I did not and have not called anyone to share the news. I know and love the God I serve. He has definite plans for my life, and they are not of harm, but of hope and an expected end (Jeremiah 29:11).

The meantime is all about perspective, attitude, and obedience. It is our time to crush the Enemy and display God well to others. I do not recall Joseph being depressed, complaining to others, questioning God, failing to step out on faith, or giving up on His purpose. Instead, he behaved as God created him to behave. He worked by using his gifts. Take that, Devil! I am following that same example. I was offered and accepted a position three business days before I was laid off. I now serve as the director of program administration for a local nonprofit organization. Before the layoff, I assumed this was a second job and was therefore an opportunity to earn additional income. But God already knew what was coming and made provision in advance. He placed me in a specifically tailored role for my gift. While the current position pays substantially less than what I was earning, I trust God to make up the slack. He has done it before and promises to do it again. I continue to serve Him in the meantime.

Are you like me? I love it when God kicks butt and allows us to see Him in action. It reminds me of the old Batman television show. When Batman and Robin fought their adversaries, the words "Pow," "Bam" or "Boom" came across the television screen as their blows landed on their foes. Joseph's endurance and commitment to his meantime tasks led him to purpose (promise).

Joseph became second in command and ruled alongside Pharaoh. Karate chop!

He saved a nation from famine. Jab!

He introduced others to God. Uppercut!

He blessed his enemies. Sucker punch!

He forgave his brothers. Headlock!

He restored his familial relationships. Drop kick!

And he was reunited with his father. Death grip!

Joseph's foes were defeated. His performance, with God's help, was a spiritual total knock out (TKO). He achieved his purpose and received God's promise. I am looking forward to the same result.

What stands out is Joseph's resolute faith in God, his unending compassion for others, and his willingness to show forth God's glory while standing on his yet-to-be-fulfilled promise. We must model this example in our meantime season. Genesis 50:30 (NIV) reads, "You intended to harm me, but God intended it for good to accomplish what is now being done, the saving of many lives." What Joseph's enemies meant for evil, God turned for his good and the saving of lives. What a powerful testimony! Whose life will you save in pursuit of promise? I dare you to crush the Enemy on the way.

Be Still, Be Open

Read and reflect on Psalm 89:20–24. Answer the questions provided below.

- Do today's devotion and biblical text references affirm for you God's faithfulness?

- List the big and small ways God continues to demonstrate to you His unfailing love and divine protection.

- Are you motivated to crush the Enemy?

- List the steps you will take this week and throughout the remainder of your meantime season to do so.

- Journal your experiences this week.

Lord, I promise _____

_____

_____

Dear God, You truly are mighty and reign supreme. Words cannot express how awestruck I am by You. Why You love me so much, I surely will never know. I am humbled and blessed to have You as my Father. Thank You for continuing to overlook my faults, for placing within me this seed, and for creating opportunities for me to succeed. Lord, I am ready and ask that You continue to walk alongside me in this season. Give me direction. I am determined to fulfill the purpose You have for me. I am committed to kicking butt in pursuit of my divine promise. I am taking this leap! Together we will crush the Enemy. In Jesus's name I pray. Amen.

CONCLUSION

I'd rather struggle than settle. Tell the devil the fight is on. The devil wants me to settle. I'm struggling not to settle for mediocrity when mightiness is calling me.

—Bishop T. D. Jakes, *The Potter's House*

"Expect the great after you leave the mountain." That was the Lord's message to me two weeks ago. It was the day after I was laid off and one year after He said I would get married. I was on my way to my church's women's retreat. Excitement was high. The participating women and I had been preparing for and looking forward to the retreat for months. Now the time had arrived. How would God move? What would He say? Expectation was indeed in the air.

Admittedly, I wondered if God would speak to me about His promise. After all, it was exactly one year ago, while in route to the last retreat, when He said I would get married. He even went so far as to describe my husband. So I wondered if, during this time, He would revisit the issue and share more with me. Just like last year, some women and I picked up the prophetess, who was serving as a guest speaker, from the airport and headed to lunch before arriving at the retreat site. Our table conversation was good, as were our meals. We paid our check and prepared to leave when the prophetess looked at me, and while tapping her wedding finger, said, "Expect the great after you leave the mountain." I flippantly said that I do not speak sign language and excused myself for the restroom. I know. I am sassy. Pray for me.

Let us take a moment to examine this message. "Expect the great after you leave the mountain." Mountains are large landforms that stretch above surrounding land. While most occur in large mountain ranges, a few occur in isolated summits. As part of the women's retreat (summit), we were consciously isolating ourselves in order to hear from God. Does this sound familiar? Moses, Elijah, and Jesus retreated to mountains (Mount Sinai, Mount Carmel, and the Mount of Olives) to hear directly from God. The Bible records the great things that occurred during and after their mountain experiences with Him. On Mount Sinai, God promised Moses that Israel would be His treasured nation if it was obedient. He further shared that Israel would be set apart as a kingdom of priests and as a holy nation. Finally, He gave Moses the Ten Commandments—the Israelites' law—on Mount Sinai. Israel was placed in covenant relationship with God. Mightiness was calling.

How about with Jesus? After fasting for forty days, Satan tempted Him. The Devil took Jesus to a high mountain, asked that Jesus serve him, and told Jesus to jump off the mountain as a challenge to see if God would save Him. Satan tried to get the Lord of Hosts to commit suicide. The Devil certainly wants us to settle. He wants to sift us as wheat. If he propositioned Jesus in this manner, we truly are not exempt. I am so glad my Lord and Savior knew better than to settle. Why would the Lord God Almighty serve Satan and forfeit destiny? Why would we? The thought is ridiculous. Mightiness was calling.

Sometime later, the Bible records that Jesus went to the Mount of Olives to petition God for His life. Understandably, He did not want to be crucified. He prayed three times that God would change His mind. Notable, however, is how Jesus ended each prayer. He ultimately prayed that God's will be done. And it was. We believers received God's promise of release from sin, redemption unto Him (salvation), the gift of the Holy Spirit, and eternal life because of Jesus's crucifixion and sacrifice. Praise God! Great things do occur after believers leave the mountains where God communes with us. Mightiness was calling.

I jokingly responded to God's message that I ought to expect the great after leaving the mountain. I, however, heard Him loud and clear and received His word. I do speak spiritual sign language. He has more in store for me. His word to me that day was His gift of aroma. It was yet another reminder to continue moving forward and not settle. It was also further confirmation that He has awesome plans for me and is taking me higher in Him. The past two years have presented moments of struggle. I will concede that, but they have been worth going through. The preceding chapters hopefully serve as a testament to this fact. Mightiness was calling.

God is faithful. And I love it when He changes His language in our favor. If you'll notice, He usually makes a promise using the word *will*. He will do x, y and z. That is how my marriage promise was given to me. However, after returning home from the retreat, God gave my pastor—who did not know what had occurred during the retreat—a new word for me. Last Sunday morning, my pastor declared that the season of waiting is over. He called to me and said my promise *is* released. God changed His language to the present. No longer is my promise resting in the future; it *is* released into my present. "Expect the great after you leave the mountain."

Alicia, what are you saying? While reading this devotional and spending time with Him, God has presented you with personal meantime activities to pursue. He is insisting that you not settle with where you are. He asks that you endure the meantime season, while heeding His instructions. He requests that you press through the struggle and stand on His word. He invites you to build His kingdom during your wait. He desires to greatly bless you. He wants to fully set you apart for His glory. He longs to fulfill His promise to you. Will you let him? Mightiness *is* calling.

ACKNOWLEDGMENTS

I thank my friend, Okater, for calling and suggesting I write a devotional. You unknowingly pushed me into a God-given assignment. I am also grateful that you read the drafts and asked questions as your way of providing feedback. You rock!

Monica, I thank you for being a friend, confidante, and mentor and for unknowingly helping me with the About the Author write-up. I had no clue of what to say. I look forward to reading your finished body of work. Do it!

To my pastors, Calvin and Camilla Smith, words cannot fully express my gratitude for you as people and godly examples. Your genuineness, integrity, and love are disarming blessings. Thank you for providing me the forum in which to grow in my walk and ministry. Thank you for investing in me, praying for me, and loving me. I am and will forever be humbled by and grateful for you. May God continue to bless, grow, and deepen your ministry.

RESOURCES

WORD TO STAND ON

The Lord is good to those who wait for Him, to the soul who seeks Him. It is good that one should hope and wait quietly for the salvation of the Lord.
—Lamentations 3:25–26 NKJV

Why are you in despair, my soul? Why are you disturbed within me? Hope in God, because I will praise Him once again, since His presence saves me and He is my God.
—Psalm 42:5 ISV

Who shall separate us from the love of Christ? Shall tribulation, or distress, or persecution, or famine, or nakedness, or peril, or sword? As it is written:

For your sake, we are killed all day long, we are accounted as sheep for the slaughter.

Yet in all these things, we are more than conquerors through Him who loved us. For I am persuaded that neither death nor life, nor angels nor principalities nor powers, nor things present nor things to come, nor height nor depth, nor any other created thing, shall be able to separate us from the love of God which is in Christ Jesus our Lord.

—Romans 8:35–39 NKJV

Do not be anxious about anything, but in every situation, by prayer and petition, with thanksgiving, present your requests to God. And the peace of God, which transcends all understanding, will guard your hearts and your minds in Christ Jesus.

—Philippians 4:6–7 NIV

Submit yourselves, then, to God. Resist the devil, and he will flee from you.

—James 4:7 NIV

Do you not know? Have you not heard? The Lord is the everlasting God, the Creator of the ends of the earth. He will not grow tired or weary, and his understanding no one can fathom. He gives strength to the weary and increases the power of the weak. Even youths grow tired and weary, and young men stumble and fall; but those who hope in the Lord will renew their strength. They will soar on wings like eagles; they will run and not grow weary, they will walk and not be faint.

—Isaiah 40:28–31 NIV

Not as though I had already attained, either were already perfect: but I follow after, if that I may apprehend that for which also I am apprehended also of Christ. Brethren I count not myself to have apprehended: but this one thing I do, forgetting those things which are behind and reaching forth unto those things which are before, I press toward

the mark for the prize of the high calling in God
in Christ Jesus.

—Philippians 3:12–14 KJV

He staggered not at the promise of God through
unbelief; but was strong in faith, giving glory to
God; and being fully persuaded that, what he had
promised, he was also able to perform.

—Romans 4:20–21 KJV

Let us draw near with a true heart in full assurance
of faith having our hearts sprinkled from an evil
conscience, and our bodies washed with pure water.
Let us hold fast the possession of our faith without
wavering; (for he is faithful that promised).

—Hebrews 10:22–23 KJV

Then Job answered the Lord, and said, I know that
thou canst do every thing, and that no thought can
be withholden from thee.

—Job 42:1–2 KJV

Now I tell you, before it come, that, when it come
to pass, ye may believe that I am he.

—John 13:19 KJV

SPIRITUAL GIFTS TESTS

Spiritual Gifts Resources—LifeWay Christian Resources
http://www.lifeway.com/lwc/files/lwcF_PDF_Discover_Your_Spiritual_Gifts.pdf

Adult Spiritual Gifts Test
http://www.spiritualgiftstest.com/test/adult

Online Spiritual Gifts Test
http://www.kodachrome.org/spiritgift/

Ministry Tools Resource Center
http://mintools.com/spiritual-gifts-test.htm

Gifted to Serve—Finding Your Place in Ministry
http://buildingchurch.net/g2s-i.htm

Online Spiritual Gifts Assessment
http://www.gregwiens.com/gifts/

PROMISE PAGES

Lord, I promise _____

_____

_____

_____

_____

_____

_____

_____

_____

_____

_____

_____

_____

_____

_____

_____

_____

_____

_____

_____

_____

_____

_____

_____

_____

_____

_____

_____

_____

_____

_____

_____

Lord, I promise _____

Lord, I promise _____

_____

_____

_____

_____

_____

_____

_____

_____

_____

_____

_____

_____

_____

_____

_____

_____

_____

_____

_____

_____

_____

_____

_____

_____

_____

_____

_____

_____

_____

_____

_____

_____

Lord, I promise _____

Lord, I promise _____

_____
_____
_____
_____
_____
_____
_____
_____
_____
_____
_____
_____
_____
_____
_____
_____
_____
_____
_____
_____
_____
_____
_____
_____
_____
_____
_____
_____
_____

ABOUT THE AUTHOR

Alicia lives in Washington, DC, and is the parent of a college-age son. She serves in ministry at one of the fastest-growing prophetic, family-based ministries in the Washington metropolitan area. She is joyful, energetic, enterprising, and sassy. In terms of spiritual gifts, Alicia embodies the gift of administration, which she uses professionally and for the building of God's kingdom.

Alicia earned a graduate degree in urban planning and policy from the University of Illinois at Chicago and an undergraduate degree in broadcast journalism from Syracuse University. Though quite astute, she is likewise adventurous and cultured. Alicia is a foodie and loves the arts, the outdoors, traveling, and reading. She is also a consummate learner.

Printed in the United States
By Bookmasters